easy green

The Absolute Easiest Ways
to Preserve Your Earth

Belma Michael Johnson

easy green

The Absolute Easiest Ways
to Preserve Your Earth

Chicago Host of HGTV's *Designed to Sell*

DreamBooks
Burbank, California, U.S.A.

www.EasyGreenBook.com

Johnson, Belma Michael
Easy Green: The Absolute Easiest Ways to Preserve Your
Earth / Belma Michael Johnson

Cover design by Peri Poloni-Gabriel, Knockout Design,
www.knockoutbooks.com

Interior design by John R. Webster & Francie Droll,
Abacus Graphics, www.abacusgraphics.com

Includes bibliographical references.

1. Environmental protection – Citizen participation.
      2. Environmentalism
      I. Johnson, Belma   II. Title

ISBN 978-0-9701527-0-1

Printed in the United States of America

10 9 8 7 6 5 4 3 2 1

First Edition

"Green is the prime color of the world, and that from which its loveliness arises."

— Pedro Calderon de la Barca

CONTENTS

MAKING & INVESTING EASY GREEN   133

A FINAL THOUGHT   149

"We are prone to speak of the resources of this country as inexhaustible; this is not so."

— President Theodore Roosevelt

What I am about to say is personal. It's about you. Your life. Your earth.

This book is about how you can do your part to preserve your earth. Easily.

To begin, each of us must answer for ourselves: How green am I? How green do I want to be?

I see three basic shades.

At one extreme, there's Ed Begley, my fellow host on HGTV. He's an activist. He's committed. He's borderline fanatical about his green. If you've ever watched an episode of "Living with Ed" on HGTV, you know exactly what I mean. He drives an electric car. He uses pedal-power to generate energy for his home to function. He is all-green all the time. He's a green legend.

I call that dark green.

At the other end of the spectrum is a woman I once met on an airplane. She was militantly against everything green. She swore that she'd drive her SUV until Armageddon, even if driving her SUV caused Armageddon. She's what I call pale green.

My uneducated guess is that 1% of us are dark green (committed activists), and 1% of us are pale green (violently opposed to the green movement).

This book is for the 98% in between. We can't imagine ourselves dark green. We don't see ourselves as pale green. We're looking for light green.

Easy Green.

We'd prefer to do what's good for our health and the health of the planet, as long as we don't have to bust our budget or bust our buttocks to do it. We've noticed that some greenness can be too time-consuming, too expensive, too burdensome, or just plain too tacky. We don't want our homes to be common or uncomfortable, and we don't want to give up our favorite creature comforts, just so we can say we're green.

And please don't lay a guilt trip on us, or a snake-oil sales pitch, or bogus science. Take it easy. We want Easy Green.

This book is easy in five different ways.

Easy on the mind. Not a lot to read. Not a lot of scientific vocabulary and intricate detail. You can read any chapter in five minutes.

Easy on the time. It's a short list of easy actions anyone can take quickly to become greener.

Easy on the wallet. You can do almost anything in this book for free, or for cheap, or for cheaper than the alternatives, or—at worse—for cheaper in the long run.

Easy on the Earth. This is a thin book because thick books eat up your trees and your time. Also, by using a 21st century printing method, the copy of this book that you're holding was probably printed after you ordered it. This is because creating, storing and transporting a massive inventory of books is primitive and wasteful. Finally, this book is sold primarily online because it takes so many natural resources to get books to bookstores. (If you'd like, you can order this book at any bookstore in the world. We'd just prefer that you help us usher in a new era of book publishing.)

Easy on the politics. Here's my feeling on the matter: Regardless if you are from a blue state or a red state, most of us like the green parts of our state and would like them to renew themselves so that they stay green. Being green isn't partisan. It's enlightened self-interest. Not about politics or personalities.

Green is good. It's good to make the most of any valuable possession. It's good to save money. It's good to leave the earth better than we found it. It's good to make healthy choices. Simple as that. In this book, green simply means healthy for our bodies and healthy for our planet.

So, relax. You won't be asked to spend thousands of dollars replacing all your windows or to heat your home exclusively with photovoltaic technology. Those ideas may have merit, but those are dark-green ideas. There are plenty of books on that. Inside these pages, you'll finally find what many of us have been looking for: something you can do right now; something that won't cost you a lot of time or money that, frankly, you do not have or do not care to spend. In this book, you'll find a lighter shade of green.

Easy Green.

"One touch of Nature makes the whole world kin."

— William Shakespeare

Introduction

~~~~~~

"*The future is not a gift—it is an achievement.*"

<div align="right">

— Harry Lauder,
20th century Scottish entertainer

</div>

I love that philosophy. It's inspiring. It's true.

I cannot believe a politician said it. Harry Lauder (the originator of the statement) wasn't a politician, so far as I know. But Stephen Johnson (who quoted him) is a powerful politician. He's the head of the Environmental Protection Agency (EPA) in the George W. Bush administration.

Many environmentalists hate the Bush administration policies regarding the environment. As I promised in the preface, I won't get into politics. I'm not qualified to do so, there are plenty of people who are quite willing to have those arguments with you, and that is not the purpose of this book. I want to point out the common ground…the areas where we all agree…the harmonies in the public dialog. And the truth is that the politician is right.

The future is not a gift—it is an achievement.

It is also true that there are EPA employees all over this country who are true and right. I do not only mean employees of the federal EPA. All 50 states have EPAs. They have great information about how you can do your part. Many of the tips in this book are drawn from the websites and other public information generated by the EPAs across America. It's terrific information. Some of their advice is hard to follow. But much of it is really quite easy. I, of course, have scoured their websites to find the Easy Green. But I suggest you visit the site for your state because there's a lot of cool stuff there. If you live in Alabama, they have a water wheel that teaches you over 20 different ways to save water in about five minutes. It's a fun teaching tool. And they'll probably send you one for free. It's easy to read and its tips are easy to do. They show you how you can do your part and take it easy at the same time. To see what I mean, just go to **www.legacyenved.org**. Or go to **www.EasyGreen-Book.com** and you'll find links to all 52 EPAs (one for all 50 states, the district of Columbia and the federal EPA). Our taxes paid for their research, so we might as well put it to use. Otherwise, the whole thing is a waste. And the earth suffers. Of course, your other option is to flip through the pages of this book because I think I've picked the best best ideas from them all and made them easy to understand. Easy to do.

The future is not a gift—it is an achievement.

In other words, whatever happens will happen because of what we do. Let's stop focusing on what might happen or might not happen to the earth if we do not act. Let's focus on what will happen to the earth when we do act. That's an idea everybody, on both sides of the argument, can agree on. Here's some more of what Stephen Johnson had to say.

"At EPA, we believe that environmental responsibility is everyone's responsibility. Thankfully, our citizens are getting the message. From newspaper headlines to the covers of Fortune 500 reports, we are reading about more and more companies, communities and individuals working to outdo each other in going 'green.' The United States is shifting to a 'green culture.' So now, instead of having only 17,000 EPA employees working to protect the environment, we have 300 million Americans as environmental partners. And that's just here at home.

'The future is not a gift - it is an achievement.' By serving causes larger than yourself, you will not only enrich your life, you will help create a more hopeful future for us all."

Stephen Johnson,
Environmental Protection Agency Administrator
May 5, 2007

Stephen Johnson agrees that we all need to play a role in improving the earth. He believes in the principles that I call Easy Green.

Others believe, too.

You've probably noticed that a number of celebrities talk about preserving the earth. Actually, they talk about saving the earth, which is a more dramatic way of saying it. You would expect actors to be more dramatic.

I can't think of two actors more different than Arnold Schwarzenegger (now appearing in the role of California Governor) and Leonardo DiCaprio (the force behind an environmental film called, "The 11th Hour.")

Just picture them: Arnold & Leo. Complete opposites. In every way.

Except when it comes to the topic of Easy Green.

The debate is over, the science is in, the time to act is now. —**Arnold**

"Thousands of climate scientists agree that global warming is not only the most threatening environmental problem, but one of the greatest challenges facing all of humanity." —**Leo**

"Mainstream scientists are convinced, mainstream CEOs are convinced, and if you look at the surveys, mainstream Americans are convinced that global warming and climate change is real and we have to do something about it. So who are the fanatics now? They are the ones who are in denial. They're in environmental denial, they're in economic denial, and they are in political denial." —**Arnold**

"The fact is we are pumping way too much carbon dioxide from our cars, refineries and power plants into the atmosphere much faster than the land and seas can absorb it. The accumulating gas is trapping heat and upsetting the world's climate." —**Leo**

"The new environmental movement is not about guilt, it's not about fringe, and it's not about being overwhelmed by the enormity of the problem, but it is about mainstream momentum." —**Arnold**

"The environmental age is here. Let's reduce our dependency on oil, foreign and domestic. Let's develop a global politics that accelerates the transition to clean fuels and sustainable energy from renewable sources." —**Leo**

"I don't think that any movement has ever made much progress based on guilt. Guilt is passive, guilt is inhibiting, and guilt is defensive. Successful movements are not built on guilt. They're built on passion, they're built on confidence, and they're built on critical mass." —**Arnold**

"Let's set an example now for future generations and move environmentalism from being the philosophy of a passionate minority to a way of life that automatically integrates ecology into governmental policy and normal living standards." —**Leo**

"The environmental movement is about to get to the tipping point. I believe the tipping point will be occurring when the environmental movement is no longer seen as a nag or as a scold, but as a positive force in people's lives." —**Arnold**

"You don't have to be a lawmaker, scientist, or in the White House to take action to protect the environment. Reduce your own impact on the environment in your daily lives. Most importantly, get educated about local, state and national politicians and their environmental policies." —**Leo**

"I believe the environmental movement is in the midst of redefining itself as something more modern, more confident, and more positive." —**Arnold**

"Individual action is critically important, as we can make decisions in our daily lives that can change the planet little by little." —**Leo**

These two different men, with different approaches and different political views, agree on certain principles: that we all need to work together, that the time to act is now, and that small changes by massive numbers of people will make a big difference. Those are the principles of Easy Green. This book is designed to show you small steps we can take to cover a great distance in a short time. We'll let the politicians and activists worry about the big problems and the hard decisions.

Meanwhile, as the experts argue, the rest of us will take small steps alone and make great progress together.

Foreword

"Individual action from every American can add up to a tremendous collective effort, and can produce significant results."

— Samuel Bodman,
U.S. Secretary of the Department of Energy
October, 2005

As he promoted a nationwide campaign called "Easy Ways to Save Energy," the Energy Secretary unwittingly summarized the philosophy of this book.

Essentially, he said small acts by millions of people make a big difference. He even had his department put together a brochure and campaign to help American families and businesses learn how to help the earth and help themselves at the same time.

They gave away "Energy $avers Guide" in person and online. Free tips…all about how you can save money and save the earth. (You can still get your copy at **www. EnergySavers.gov**.)

The information is out there. Our state and federal governments are doing a fantastic job of collecting information about saving the earth. There are brilliant ideas all over the web. There are hundreds of brochures and what-not that you can get in the mail—for free. But who's reading it?

Not enough of us.

That's why I wrote this book. To collect the best of the public information in one place, one book—that's easy to read.

Any chapter of this book can change your life.

Start anywhere. Just pick any area of your life, flip to that chapter and find out how you can live greener.

I promise: you can finish any chapter in five minutes— or less.

Give me five minutes a day for 30 days and I promise to green-up your entire life. Just read a chapter and choose one tip to follow. In one month, you'll have 30 easy, new habits that will help preserve your earth in all areas of your life.

Easy changes. Easy decisions. Easy Green.

Why does this book contain only easy solutions? So that everyone will participate. There are 300 million Americans. When we move as a unit, we change the world—for better or worse. When Americans all chipped in a dime, we cured polio. Practically wiped it from the face of the earth. Now let's do something for the face of the earth.

Individual action from every American will add up to a tremendous collective effort.

We will change the world.

Easy …

Acknowledgments

~~~~~~

In all my books, I thank my wife Tammy first. If you saw what I'm like when I'm writing a book, you would understand. (Even an easy book like this one takes over your life.) I also need to thank my brother Charles, who helped me develop this idea and who edited every word.

Thanks to my friend Mark Gill for inviting me to Paris last Christmas, where I saw how another country thinks about the environment. I wondered what would happen if a country as big as America got serious about preserving the earth. I am convinced we can change the world if we put forth even a little effort in the same direction.

Thank you to my friends at HGTV for giving me this opportunity to make a difference. Thanks to Ed Begley for bringing our entire network into the green universe by the sheer force of his passion and personality. Thanks to Ken Lowe, Judy Girard, Michael Dingley, Melissa Sykes, Maddie Henri, Mary Ellen Iwata, Andy Singer,

Gabriella Messina, Bill Myers, Amy Quimby, Steve Lewis, Audrey Adlam, Emily Yarborough, Dynell Searight, Amy Gibson Hammontree, and the executive directly responsible for my show, "Designed to Sell," Laura Sillars. I believe HGTV can and will inspire American homeowners to think green, spend green and live green in their homes.

Thank you, my friend, Clive Pearse and, my friend, Lisa LaPorta for making "Designed to Sell" a success. Thank you a thousand times.

Thank you to the geniuses who created the show and gave me an opportunity to participate in it—the founders of Pie Town Productions: Tara Sandler, Jennifer Davidson, and Scott Templeton. Greg Spring, who championed me to the founders. And to the team of senior producers I work with: Beth Suskin, Todd Pflughoeft, Sarah Patten, Jennifer Bernardi, Betsy Allman, Dana Besnoy, Samantha Leonard, Alicia Conway, Amy Arthun, Dezhda Gaubert, Anna Butler and Cat Pasciak.

And thank you to my "Designed to Sell" co-stars in Chicago: Chad Lopez, Brandie Malay, Robert North, Monica Pedersen, and Bethany Souza, as well as the rest of my "DTS-Chicago" family. I also must acknowledge my "DTS" siblings in Washington, D.C., Taniya Nayak and Shane Tallant. Thank you Marc Kamler and Chelsea Spurlock for all you do. Thank you to Dr. James Stoxen for healing the crick in my neck that writing a book can cause.

Thank you to all the Home Show Producers across America who have helped me get this message out by inviting me to speak at your events. Thank you to my friends Vikki Prudden, the Honorable State Sen. Sylvia Anderson and everybody at National Exhibitions & Communications Group for being the first to let me share this message. You inspired this book. Thank you to all my friends at dmg world media, International Exhibitions and American Consumer Shows for your continuing support.

Thank you to my creative collaborators Charles Anthony Johnson, my friend and book cover designer Peri Gabriel, and my new friends and book interior designers John R. Webster and Francie Droll. I literally could not have done this without you.

THE EASY GREEN HOME

According to the U.S. Department of Energy, the average existing home consumes 100 million BTUs of energy per year. I'm not exactly sure what a BTU is, but I sure don't remember using 100 million of them last year. I am quite sure that I would like to cut that number down this year. But…I'd like to do it the easy way.

Besides reducing the enormous amount of energy our homes consume, there's another important opportunity that's literally at our doorstep: green home improvement. Every week on "Designed to Sell," we help people improve their homes. More and more on our network, we're becoming aware of the green options available for these upgrades.

Consider this: Every year the American homeowner spends $300 billion on home improvements. What if all that money were working for the earth, rather than against it? The American homeowner literally could change the world.

Now you see why, at HGTV, we have a saying: Start at home.

When you're looking for easy ways to preserve the earth, I would say: Start in the kitchen.

THE EASY GREEN HOME

Easy Green Kitchen

Let's take a tour around your kitchen, beginning with your sink.

Do not wash dishes by hand. Yes! I love this advice because now I can feel good about being lazy. Washing dishes by hand actually eats up more energy than using an automatic dishwasher...more of the earth's energy and more of your energy. So let the dishwasher do the dirty work. It's easier. And it's greener.

Buy green. When you buy a dishwasher, look for an Energy Star model. (The EPA and U.S. Department of Energy do all the work of testing, measuring, and rating the dishwashers. All you have to do is buy one they designate an Energy Star. Easy!)

Green hand-washing. If you live in an older home where adding a dishwasher would be an outrageous expense, try to limit your water use by filling up one pan with soapy water and another with rinse water.

Rinse now. Swish those leftovers off the plate right away. You'll waste two gallons of hot water to get that petrified steak juice or those hardened fruit stains off the plate two days (or even two hours) from now.

Go low-flow. A low-flow aerator uses less than half the water and less energy than a standard aerator. (An aerator is the little gizmo on the tip of your faucet. Replace the gizmo once and your kitchen is green forever! Easy.)

Use cold water. When you wash your hands, or clean fruit, or rinse a dish, use cold water instead of hot. Saves energy, prevents carbon emissions.

Keep a bowl in the sink. Capture that once-used cold water and re-use it to water plants.

Refrigerate later. Don't put hot leftovers in the fridge. Let them cool off first. Just think, "Simma down now. Refrigerate later." Be smart: you don't want to leave meat, poultry or eggs sitting around more than an hour. (Green is good. But not green meat.)

Do the dollar bill test. Take a one dollar bill and lodge it in your refrigerator door, half inside and half out. Close the door. Now pull the dollar out. If the dollar escapes too easily, you need to adjust the latch, replace the seal or buy a new Energy Star fridge because many dollars are escaping through that door every month in the form of wasted energy.

Fill the fridge. An empty fridge has to work harder to keep its contents cool because food holds onto its coolness better than air does. Don't be ridiculous (like my mother and mother-in-law) and overstuff your refrigerator, though. Air must circulate in a fridge for cooling to take place. So, moms, please let your fridge breathe a little! Please. (Close down the Museum of Jurassic peas in the freezer.)

Blue is better. If you have a natural-gas range, take a look at the flame it produces. A blue flame means you're in good shape. A yellow flame means your gas is burning inefficiently. You can fix this problem either with the manufacturer of the appliance or with your local utility company.

Clean those burners. We all spill food on the burners. That's understandable. The problem is leaving them dirty. They burn inefficiently when they're caked with spaghetti sauce or other crud. Give them a good scrub.

Boil better. Cover a pot or pan when you're boiling water. All that steam is wasted energy.

Cook faster. Use microwave ovens, toaster ovens, electric pans and pressure cookers instead of your oven whenever you can.

Forget the doors. If you're designing a new kitchen or thinking of replacing your cabinet doors, consider this: go doorless. Open cabinets use less wood and provide easier access. (Downside: you can't have messy cabinets.)

Take nothing for granite. If you're replacing your granite countertop, don't just throw it away...give it away. Someone may be able to use your leftover granite for a smaller home project. Donate your granite to a company that sells remnants. (Besides being a really good Easy Green tip; I love the word play: "Take nothing for granite." Hilarious.)

Get medieval. Consider using a hand tool for easy chopping, grinding, mixing and grating. I do so little cooking that this is Easy Green for me. If you cook more, then think about using the manual tools for small meals or on weekends.

Take off your shoes. A healthy kitchen is a green kitchen. More than 60% of the dust and dirt in your kitchen walks in the door on the bottom of your shoes. Leave the dirt and the shoes outside. Easy!

Kitchens use a lot of energy (10 to 15 percent of the total household energy is sucked up by refrigerators and freezers alone). Doing anything on the above list is better than doing nothing. If you can't part with your Cuisinart, at least take off your shoes. Or your cabinet doors.

If you have good Easy Green ideas for the kitchen, submit them at **www.EasyGreenBook.com.** Click on the link entitled "The Green Team."

THE EASY GREEN HOME

Easy Green Bath

Flushing the toilet uses almost one-third of all the water consumed by a typical household. And, remember, toilets use fresh water—the kind of water we drink. Only three percent of all the water on earth is fresh water, and that includes the two-thirds that is frozen in glaciers and polar caps. So, really, we all have to survive on one percent of the water on earth. Hmmm. Seems like we would want to waste as little as possible on flushing the toilet and such. Here are some other green things to think about in your bathroom.

Showers are greener than baths. Even though the water is not running while you clean yourself, a typical bath uses almost twice as much water as a typical shower. The exception is the "power shower"—those wasteful devices that perform water acrobatics so your muscles can feel that pulsating sensation as you rinse. Those showers use even more water than a bath. Try this: have a short shower and a long massage.

The five-minute rule. I know, I know. A morning shower is part of my ritual, too. It's how I wake up. I need to make the transition from a warm bed to a warm shower. But 10 minutes is too long. Did you know that mom, dad, sister and brother use 1,400 gallons of water every week, just by taking 10-minute showers? By cutting that in half you save enough water to fill a swimming pool—every week. You also save the carbon emissions that it takes to heat the extra water.

Go low-flow in the shower. Shorter showers cut water consumption in half, but low-flow shower heads cut that amount in half again. Green house gases are reduced. Energy bills go down. Water bills dry up. What's easier or greener than that?

Get hip to hemp. Consider switching to a hemp shower curtain. Hemp is more eco-friendly than vinyl and fights mildew better.

Go low-flow at the bowl. What uses the most water in your home? Yep, the toilet. In the U.S., we flush away almost five billion gallons of water every day. You flush down 9,000 gallons per year by yourself. With a low-flow device, you're helping the planet with every flush.

A toilet bowl is not a trash can. How many times have you flushed down a single ply of tissue paper with three gallons of water? Stop the madness! This is an easy way to be greener.

Message in a Bottle...in the Toilet. Send a message in a bottle to Mother Nature. Tell her you love her by putting a weighted bottle in your toilet tank to displace the water that would be wasted on your next flush.

Join the leak police. We have 600 million eyeballs in this country. If we use them to look for leaks in our homes, at our friends' homes, at our jobs, and wherever else we go, we can stop one of the biggest water-wasters on the planet—the fixable leak. Devote at least one eye to looking for leaks and one lip to reporting them.

Open a window. The natural light will illuminate your bathroom more efficiently and the natural ventilation is crucial to healthy air quality.

Grey is green. Capturing grey water—that's water used once before—and using it again is an easy way to cut your water use in half. Shower water can be re-used to water plants, or mop, or wash windows, or to loosen up that stain on the driveway. It's easier for us to find creative ways to re-use water, than it is to find new sources of water we can use.

If you have good Easy Green ideas for the bathroom, submit them at **www.EasyGreenBook.com.** Click on the link entitled "The Green Team."

THE EASY GREEN HOME

~~~~~~~~~~~~~~~~~~~~~~~~~~~~~~~~~~~~

Easy Green Bedroom

"*What is the use of a house if you haven't got a tolerable planet to put it on?*"

— Henry David Thoreau

Take a deep breath. How does your bedroom smell? Be honest! We're often so conscious of the temperature in our bedrooms that we don't think about the air quality. People: A bedroom needs fresh air—regularly. Even in the hot summer and cold winter. We cannot live on heat or air conditioning alone! And now for a little more bedroom advice…

Recycle your bedding. Old sheets, duvets, covers, throws and bedspreads can live on as sewing projects. If you don't sew, it's easy to find a sewing group online that does. Make a donation!

Beware of the pillow. Besides the obvious perils of pillow fighting, we don't usually imagine much danger coming from that fluffy, comfy companion resting beneath our sleeping heads. Think about it: People perspire. Pillows absorb. Moisture sits. Mustiness happens. Mold develops. Suddenly, you're resting your head on a puffy Petri dish every night—and you wonder why you're congested. Not good. Easy fixes: Buy organic bedding. Frequently check for mold. And let a little sunlight and air hit your pillows every once in a while. Green living means healthy living.

Counting sheets. Yes, when you're adding up your green score in the bedroom, sheets count too. They absorb sweat from your entire body, all night long, every night. (Plus, the body of whomever or whatever you sleep with.) First, know your allergies. It is definitely not green to sleep on a fiber that makes you sick. Organic cotton is ideal for the winter. Linen is the top summer choice. Whereas polyester is petroleum-based. Not green. Many of those no-iron finishes contain toxins. Not green. And silk sheets need dry cleaning, which requires unhealthy chemicals. Definitely not green.

What's in your mattress? Most likely you're sleeping on a bed of fire retardants or pesticides. Polyurethane foam is usually fire-proofed. Wool is made from sheep that are treated with pesticides to prevent parasites. Easy fix: invest in an organic wool mattress. I know, this isn't cheap. But, come on: how often do you replace your mattress? Maybe every ten years? This counts as Easy Green just because one change makes your bed greener for a decade. We will change the world...one mattress at a time.

What's in your closet? A source of unhealthy air may be lurking in your closet. Be sure to air-dry dirty towels before storing them in a hamper. Moisture can lead to mold, which can lead to colds, asthma or worse. Every so often, leave your doors open to increase airflow.

Design to Smell. Use your nose to hunt down problem areas in your bedroom. Stale air can lead to mold. Anywhere you find mold developing, clear the area of furniture near that wall. Your goal is to increase airflow. Your second move is to call an expert to professionally investigate the problem.

Forecast: humid and clear. If you use a humidifier, keep the device and the water it contains clean. Follow the manufacturer's instructions carefully. You don't want to circulate unhealthy air.

If you have good Easy Green ideas for the bedroom, submit them at **www.EasyGreenBook.com.** Click on the link entitled "The Green Team."

THE EASY GREEN HOME

~~~~~~~~~~~~~~~~~~~~~~~~~~~~~~~~

Green Light

If you're remotely interested in green living, you've heard the familiar pitch for CFLs: Compact Fluorescent bulbs. They cost a little more, but they last a lot longer. In fact, some people like using the bulbs outdoors because of their longevity. They also give off less heat, so you can use less energy cooling the room where you use them. They only use 25 percent of the energy that the common incandescent bulb does. An estimated 95% of the power eaten up by incandescent bulbs produces heat, instead of light. Those are all pretty compelling reasons to pick up a CFL. But here's the one that got me: if every U.S. household replaced just one bulb, the reduction in pollution would be equivalent to removing one million cars off the road. Imagine if we all replaced TWO bulbs...or ALL of our incandescent bulbs. But let's not get ahead of ourselves: one bulb...that's all we ask. (Preferably one in a room that you use often.)

Don't be dim. My friend Jeff said he doesn't use CFLs because they're too dim. I asked about that problem at a lighting store. Here's what they told me: A 20-watt CFL produces as much light as a 100-watt incandescent. You may have to ask a question to get the right bulb. As it turns out, Jeff, it wasn't the bulb that was dim.

Dim and dimmer. If you can get away with it, use dimmer switches and lower-wattage bulbs in hallways, on stairways and landings.

Your dad was right. Turn out the lights when no one is in the room. Duh! This is the most ridiculously Easy-Green solution of all. So why don't we—and, yes, that includes me—why don't we do this? I have to insist that everyone form this habit. If it helps, put a picture of your dad by every light switch. Seriously, the average home in America generates two-thirds of a ton of greenhouse gases just from lighting every year.

> *Due to improvements in fluorescent technology, it is no longer true that it takes more energy to turn lights off and on than it takes to keep them running. With the modern advancements, the wise move is turn off the lights when you're not using them.*
>
> Source: "Home Energy Saver,"
> Department of Energy

The best things in light are free. Daylight is the greenest light around. Better even than compact fluorescents. Sunlight gives you much more than just illumination.

Sunlight feeds the body, plants, animals and the soul. Let the sun light up your life.

A higher power. Yes, signing up for "green" power will probably make your power bill go higher. But it also will mean that your home is being fed by wind power or solar energy. Sooner or later, if enough of us sign up, the cost charged to our households will go down. But even if only you sign up, the cost charged to the earth goes down immediately. Please ask your utility company about signing up for green power.

The seven year switch. Imagine a bulb that lasts 10,000 hours—a full seven years of normal usage! This is possible now. All you need is an Energy Star fixture. To qualify for this distinction, the fixtures must use one-third as much energy as traditional lighting. They come in all sorts of types and flavors, so you don't have to sacrifice your light style to save money and energy. See the light …fixture!

Sensors and sensibility. Green doesn't get easier than this: use motion sensors. After your initial investment, all you have to do is leave the room to be green. Or sit very still. You can actually improve the environment while taking a nap. (Assuming you don't toss and turn.)

Let night lights be night lights. Parents have been leaving porch lights on for their late-arriving children since Fred Flinstone's day. These days, generating electricity is our greatest contributor to carbon dioxide emissions. All those night lights add up. So turn them off in the daytime. Or better yet, put them on one of those cheap little timers. (And see if you can get away with a 9-watt CFL bulb.)

The glorious South. In Chicago, I have an apartment with four large south-facing windows. As a result, I'm flooded with sunlight throughout most of the year. Even in the fiercely famous Chicago winter, I only had to use my heater a total of two hours — all winter! Use your south-facing windows to warm up your place. They are the best! (Unless, you live in Australia, in which case it's north-facing windows.)

Light is right. If you're flipping a coin about whether to paint a room a neutral light color or a dark accent color, consider this: light colors reflect light, which means you can illuminate the room for less money forever just by picking the lighter shade. So if it's all the same to you …

> *According to the National Park Service: "Bad lights do more than just spoil the view of the stars, they can confuse and harm wildlife, create light trespass, waste energy, create glare, and actually reduce nighttime visibility. Bad lights often cost less to purchase and install, but end up costing much more in the lifetime of the fixture."*

If you have good Easy Green ideas for household lighting, submit them at **www.EasyGreenBook.com.** Click on the link entitled "The Green Team."

THE EASY GREEN HOME

Cool Green & Green Heat

It always seems to be too hot or too cold. At home, that's just not acceptable. Home should be homey...comfortable. But at what cost? We use more than half the energy that our homes consume on heating and cooling. As individual homeowners, we are not doing much damage to the environment, but altogether the cooling and heating systems in American homes emit 150 million tons of carbon dioxide into the environment every year. It's the biggest piece of the energy pie. Use the following suggestions to judge your coolness...and your heating habits.

See the light! Move lights away from your air conditioning thermostat because they'll trick the cooler into runner longer than necessary.

Go duct hunting. Your air ducts are potential energy-savers. Seal any holes and look for sections that should be adjoined. Get your ducts in order!

Warm returns. Because of the rate of heat transfer, it actually takes more energy to keep your house warm than it does to warm it up when you return home, assuming you keep your thermostat set around 72 degrees when the outside temperature is 40 degrees or colder. This means, in colder climates, you'll save money and energy by turning off the heat when you're away and turning it back on when you return.

Beware of the filthy filter. A clean filter is cheap. A dirty filter costs you money every day and costs the earth unnecessary energy. Don't let filters be out of mind just because they're out of sight. Replace the filter every time you pay the bill and you should see the monthly bill grow smaller.

Fan appreciation. A good fan is more efficient than air conditioning. (A whole-house fan uses 20% less energy than a central air conditioner.) Quite often, to feel cooler, all you need is moving air. If it's just you at home and you don't want to refrigerate the whole house, you may want to consider a battery-operated fan that automatically shuts off after a set time. (Extra points if you use rechargeable batteries.) And in the winter, a fan running in reverse pushes warm air down to where the people are. So turn off the air conditioning thermostat and turn on the fans.

> *Many people refuse to turn off their water heater because they believe it takes more energy to heat up the water they need than it would take to keep the water warm. This is a myth. Turning off the water heater for a few hours each day actually saves energy.*
>
> Source: "Home Energy Saver,"
> Department of Energy

Follow the sun. As a habit, open shades and curtains when the sun in shining in the wintertime. Habitually, close them when the sun goes down. Better to spend a little of your energy every day than waste the sun's energy all day.

Full loads only. Make sure you only run your washing machine, dryer and dishwasher with full loads.

> *Dirty insulation often indicates the holes where air is leaking in or out of your house.*
>
> Source: Free, downloadable ENERGY SAVERS:
> Tips on Saving Energy and Money at Home

Green layout. Here's a design challenge: see if there's an aesthetic way to position your favorite seating near windows that give you good natural light and warmth. You'll save two types of energy (lighting and heating), curb emissions and enjoy the healthy effects of the sun.

Follow the smoke. To check your home for insulation problems, light a stick of incense. Hold it near windows, doors, electrical boxes and outlets, plumbing and ceiling fixtures, attic hatches and anywhere else that you think air could be escaping. If the smoke moves horizontally, you've found a leak that you should seal. If it doesn't...at least you've made the room smell more pleasant.

> *If you are annoyed that certain rooms in your home are always hot or always cold, no matter what you do, the culprits probably are bad air ducts, poor insulation or inefficient windows.*
> Source: "Home Energy Saver,"
> Department of Energy

Hot summer nights. During the summer, run your heat-producing appliances (washers, dryers, dishwashers, vacuum cleaners) at night when it's cooler. I can't think of a better reason to procrastinate on your chores.

It's always flue season. All seasons of the year, remember to manage your fireplace flue. The fireplace is often the last place we look for the hole in the house that makes it difficult to control the temperature. The flue lets warm air escape in the winter and cool air escape in the summer.

Cover the pool. If you heat an outside pool, cover it every night. Otherwise 40 to 70 percent of your energy will go up in steam. Bad for your wallet, bad for the earth.

> *Many people are convinced that they'll have to wait a few minutes to take a warm shower if they turn off their water heater during the day to save energy. This is a myth. This inconvenience would materialize only if you're planning to use more water than is stored in the tank.*
>
> Source: "Home Energy Saver,"
> Department of Energy

If you have good Easy Green ideas for cooling or heating your home, submit them at **www.EasyGreenBook.com**. Click on the link entitled "The Green Team."

THE EASY GREEN HOME

~~~~~~~~~~~~~~~~~~~~~~~~~~

Easy Green Furniture

"*The finest workers in stone are not copper or steel tools, but the gentle touches of air and water working at their leisure with a liberal allowance of time.*"

— Henry David Thoreau

You probably don't think about your furniture in terms of its greenness…but you should. If we're going to turn our respective countries and, eventually, the world into a great, big green machine, it's going to have a lot of tiny, little moving parts. The goal of the Easy Green approach is to give everything in our lives a tint of green so that no particular aspect has to be too green. All in favor of this plan, read on.

What's in your furniture? Think of yourself as putting your life on a green diet. With a food diet, you have to think about the ingredients of whatever you eat. You can always tell when someone's dieting because whenever they're offered food, they ask, "What's in it?" The same principle applies to someone who's greening. When they look at furniture, for instance, they want to know what materials were used. If you're going to join the Green Team, you want to start thinking this way. I know it's a cliché—OK, an annoying cliché—to say we need to protect trees. But we do! Remember third grade? Trees produce oxygen, and they absorb carbon dioxide. They're our breathing partners. They clean a lot of the crud out of the sky that we put there. They also cool off the planet...the same planet that many people believe we're accidentally warming up. The roots from trees literally hold the earth together. Animals live in trees. They live off trees. They live under trees. And, besides, everyone has a fond childhood memory of a friendly neighborhood tree. We climb them and carve them. Their wood warms our homes, they are a source of shade from the heat, as well as shelter from the rain. Money doesn't grow on trees. We do. Since they've been so good to us, let's give them a little respect in return. For starters, let's stop ridiculing tree lovers. Trees are green. Green is good. Trees are good. Which brings us back to furniture. If you're buying new furniture anyway, try to buy wood that comes from forests that are harvested sustainably or from reclaimed wood.

"Walk lightly in the spring; Mother Earth is pregnant."

— Kiowa proverb

Bamboo is the new wood. Many of the qualities we love about wood can be found in bamboo. But bamboo is a form of grass and so it replenishes much faster than trees. Perhaps most important: it's beautiful. Look for bamboo furniture. Fall in love with it. The planet will thank you.

An old answer. One of the best ways to go green with your furniture is to buy stuff that already exists. Believe me, the world has plenty of furniture in it already. It's now chic to buy a pre-owned Mercedes or BMW. Pre-owned furniture is just as good: seriously consider hand-me-downs, vintage accessories, or exquisite antiques. Good taste, and good for the planet.

Believe in afterlife! The new life cycle of furniture is cradle to cradle, instead of cradle to grave. Many of today's artisans are intentionally building furniture that can be easily made into something else later. Here's the key question: how easily can you dissemble it? If it's easier to take apart, it's easier to re-use.

Be green inside and out. When shopping for outside furniture, lean toward products made from recycled wood or metal. Buying one recycled bench spares our landfills an amount of waste equal to two thousand plastic bottles.

Buy locally. In our modern world, we're capable of buying anything we want from any part of the world. But should we? Do we need to? Every time? The costs of shipping are greater than just the freight or postage costs. Weigh the environmental costs of air travel or truck transport. Is that lamp really worth that much to you? Couldn't you try to find a lamp you like made by a local craftsman? Besides, it's in everyone's best interest to buy locally because, when we're ready to recycle our furniture, we can all sell locally.

Trash is treasure. Someone is probably looking for exactly the furniture you're throwing away. With web sites like Craig's List (**www.craigslist.org**) at our disposal, it's never been easier to pass along pre-owned furniture than right now. If you've never been to the site, it's like a global classified section. You can sell your stuff there to someone in your area or, if you can't find any interest locally, someone across the country or across an ocean. Or if you were going to throw it away anyway, advertise it under "Free Stuff." Somebody in the world could use it. Everybody is the world will benefit from your effort. Also consider eBay.com, and your local paper (or their website).

> *"If we do not permit the earth to produce beauty and joy, it will in the end not produce food either."*

— Wood Krutch, naturalist

If you have good Easy Green ideas pertaining to furniture, submit them at **www.EasyGreenBook.com**. Click on the link entitled "The Green Team."

~~~~~~~~~~~~~~~~~~~~~~~~~~~~~~~~~~~~~

Easy Green Home Office

For the first time ever, the average home includes an office. Personal computers and printers, private fax machines and copiers have become common household items. We think of our offices as perhaps the most productive room in the house. The home office also can be one of the most destructive. It's time to bring home some fiscal wisdom from the workplace.

> *In the early days, turning your personal computer off and on repeatedly was a problem. These days, your computer suffers more wear and tear from being left on continually.*
> Source: "Home Energy Saver,"
> Department of Energy

Go paperless whenever possible. Save a document on disk, or on your hard drive, or in your email box instead of printing it out and storing it in a file cabinet. Be honest, most paperwork in our home offices isn't critical. It just sits in the file cabinet. Why not let it sit in an electronic file cabinet instead? It's more convenient, cheaper and healthier for the planet.

Be a paper pincher. Squeeze as much use out a sheet of paper as possible. Print on both sides. Use shredded remains as packaging padding. (If you happen to live in Washington D.C., you should be able to find plenty of other people's shreddings. It's best to look right around election time since that tends to be peak shredding season.) Conserve paper by using smaller font sizes, whenever possible. (Often reducing a document to size 11, instead of the default size 12, will save a sheet of paper. And you'll hardly notice the difference when you're reading the document.)

Eliminate cover sheets. If you can, avoid using cover sheets for faxes. Just put a sticky note on the first page of your fax or include the recipient's name on the first page.

Cartridges are doubly evil. Printer cartridges work against us on the front end because they require important resources in order to be manufactured and they are usually discarded after their brief use, which adds to the huge heap of waste that's already weighing down the planet. What to do? Recycle. And buy recycled or refillable cartridges. Occasionally recycled cartridges don't print as clearly as new ones. They are still useful for printing jobs that don't have to be pristine, such as, boarding passes from online airline check-ins, grocery lists, maps and directions... or rough drafts of books. Have you complained that modern printers are dirt cheap, but their cartridges cost almost as much as the printer itself costs? Recycled cartridges are the solution.

Give it a rest. Keep seldom-used office equipment in sleep mode. It costs you a little time while it wakes up so you can use it. But it costs the environment all the time when you leave it turned on unnecessarily. If you are not actively printing, it's a good idea to turn your printer off. Printers use a third of their energy in stand-by mode. If you know you won't be printing all day, feel free to unplug the printer entirely.

Macintosh computers have "Energy Saver" settings. To find it, go to the Apple menu, select Control Panels and then Energy Saver.
Source: "Home Energy Saver,"
Department of Energy

Laptops are tops. Use your laptop as much as possible. (I'm using mine to write this.) And use the battery as much as possible. (I'm using mine.) A desktop pulls twice the energy out of the wall that a laptop needs. Even worse, the desktop uses a hundred times as much energy as a laptop that's operating on its battery.

Upgrade first. When you need more memory, a new chip or a more-powerful hard drive, try to upgrade your old computer rather than replacing it with a new one.

> *Most answering machines use more energy than most computers. Use voice mail.*
>
> Source: "Home Energy Saver,"
> Department of Energy

Free envelopes. You know that junk mail that comes with return envelopes? That's a resource. Cover the bar codes with ink and the pre-printed addresses with your own labels. You just saved the cost of an envelope!

> *Can you believe it? We could wrap the entire earth eight hundred times in the paper consumed by personal computers.*

If you have good Easy Green ideas for the home office, submit them at **www.EasyGreenBook.com**. Click on the link entitled "The Green Team."

~~~~~~~~~~~~~~~~~~~~~~~~~~~~~~~~~~~~

Easy Green Electronics

"When we show our respect for other living things, they respond with respect for us."

— Arapaho proverb

Give yourself a break. Instead of trashing an old piece of electronic equipment, you may be able to qualify for a tax break by donating to a worthy cause.

Upgrade. Don't be so eager to buy a new toy. See if you can upgrade your old toy, first.

Buy smart. Make sure your new electronics equipment allows for easy upgrades of hardware and memory.

Buy even smarter. Shop for equipment that is constructed with latches and snaps. You can upgrade this kind of equipment more easily and recycle it more readily.

Buy super smart. Avoid equipment that is sealed shut with glue. You can't get inside for upgrades! No glue... get a clue!

Buy extremely smart. Look for machines that use replaceable parts. Ask your salesman about this aspect of the gadget or gizmo, not just about screen size or processor speed.

Buy absolutely smart. Don't think you're getting ripped off because the equipment you're considering uses recycled materials. This is good! Green is good!

Buy ridiculously smart. Purchase equipment that uses rechargeable batteries. Every day you'll be preserving the earth just because you insisted on this feature.

Buy green. Energy Star computers use 70% less electricity than computers that have not earned that distinction. They consume less energy while you're using them and they are more efficient at rest.

No hybrids. In electronics equipment, hybrids are bad. Hybrid materials, that is. Stay away from hybrids like plastic resin. When they mix materials, it's harder to recycle. Which pile does the hybrid go in...the plastic pile or the resin pile? Answer: neither!

No excuse. The Environmental Protection Agency says there are more than 1,000 cities across the country that collect computers and electronics for recycling. There are thousands of private organizations, thousands of schools, as well as numerous county drop-off centers and even some local retailers who collect used equipment. Recycle your electronics equipment: your cell phones, your computers, your monitors, your televisions, your printers, your modems. Recycle electronics. Please.

> *More than 100 million cells phones are thrown away each year, totaling 65,000 tons of waste.*
> Source: INFORM, Inc.

Unplug! At least 75% of the energy consumed by your electronic toys is eaten up when the gadgets are off! Unplug them if you're not using them.

Stop charging the charger. When you're finished charging batteries, or your cell-phone headset, or your cell phone itself—unplug the charger. It only takes two extra seconds to first plug the gadget into the charger and then plug the charger back into the wall.

Power strip. Put your TV, DVD player, video player, computers and other electronics on a power strip so that you can turn the power strip off when you aren't using the devices.

> *Did you know the EPA has estimated that using a computer's "sleep mode" reduces its energy consumption by 60 to 70 percent and, on a large scale, ultimately could save enough electricity each year to power Vermont, New Hampshire, and Maine, cut electric bills by $2 billion, and reduce carbon dioxide emissions by the equivalent of five million cars?*

If you have good Easy Green ideas for electronics, submit them at **www.EasyGreenBook.com**. Click on the link entitled "The Green Team."

THE EASY GREEN HOME

Easy Green Gardening

"Spring would not be spring without bird songs, any more than it would be spring without buds and flowers, and I only wish that besides protecting the songsters, the birds of the grove, the orchard, the garden and the meadow, we could also protect the birds of the seashore and of the wilderness."

— President Theodore Roosevelt

Your garden should be green. And so should your gardening. Why hurt the earth as you cultivate the earth? That would make no sense at all. So take a look at this list of suggestions and ask yourself: How green is my gardening?

Sweep. One of the commonest forms of waste is when people sweep with water. Please don't use your hose to sweep your driveway. You wouldn't water your lawn with a broom, would ya?

Pull the plug. Don't use those pollutant leaf blowers either. Sweep. If you don't want to sweep, hire a neighbor's kid. That's what they're there for.

Go wild. Let the grass, plants and trees that grow naturally in your area flourish. This is easier, cheaper and less wasteful than planting and nurturing non-indigenous plant life.

> Yard waste is the single largest component of both generated waste and discarded waste.
> Source: HighBeam Research

Early or late. It's best to begin or end your day by watering your lawn. Water evaporates four to eight times faster during the heat of the day.

Think small. A lawn doesn't have to be big to be beautiful. You can give better care to a more manageable lawn and use fewer resources and less time.

"Weather means more when you have a garden. There's nothing like listening to a shower and thinking how it is soaking in around your green beans."

— Marcelene Cox, author

Let nature help. According to scientists, quite often water falls from the sky. Don't automatically water the lawn just because it's Tuesday. Check the forecast. Give yourself a reason to cheer the rain.

Start a rain collection. Catch some of that falling water in a bucket or two so that you can use it to water your garden on another day. It's like a savings account...except you're saving from a rainy day. (And saving money. And saving the earth.)

> *"Let the rain kiss you. Let the rain beat upon your head with silver beads. Let the rain sing you a lullaby."*
>
> — Langston Hughes

Don't curse the wind. There's nothing sillier than someone trying to water the lawn on a blustery day. You end up watering the driveway...the sidewalk...your shoes... the neighbor's kid ...

Sit. As often as possible, sit in your beautiful garden and just enjoy it. Read. Nap. Visit with family. Invite neighbors over. Talk. Garden sitting is one of the most unappreciated forms of entertainment on earth. It's much healthier than watching television—healthier for your soul, healthier for the planet, and healthier for your relationships.

> *Did you know if every household in the U.S. replaced just one roll of 180-sheet virgin-fiber paper towels with 100-percent recycled paper towels, we could save: 1.4 million trees, 3.7 million cubic feet of landfill space, and 526 million gallons of water, and prevent 89,400 pounds of pollution?*

If you have good Easy Green ideas for gardening, submit them at **www.EasyGreenBook.com**. Click on the link entitled "The Green Team."

THE EASY GREEN HOME

Green While You Clean

"It is also vandalism wantonly to destroy or to permit the destruction of what is beautiful in nature, whether it be a cliff, a forest, or a species of mammal or bird. Here in the United States we turn our rivers and streams into sewers and dumping-grounds, we pollute the air, we destroy forests, and exterminate fishes, birds and mammals -- not to speak of vulgarizing charming landscapes with hideous advertisements. But at last it looks as if our people were awakening."

— President Theodore Roosevelt

Our cleaning methods do harm to the earth. We don't intend to soil the earth while we clean our homes, but too often, that's exactly what we do. We can do better...easily.

Save a buck; use a bucket. Instead of running water while you scrub and clean your countertops, try rinsing them down with a bucket of water.

Move to the front. Those front-loading washing machines save more money, water and energy than top-loaders.

Air is free. The best dryer may be right in front of your eyes (even though you can't see it.) Many garments dry just as well and last longer when you simply hang them up—especially outside. I do all of my air-drying indoors. (I have no clothesline.) I find that gym clothes and tee-shirts (especially those with a design on them) much prefer to air dry. They hold their color better and fray less. Also, try air-drying wool, silk, lightweight synthetics and other delicate fabrics. Both the garments and the earth will thank you. And so will I.

Air is free—part II. Shut off your dishwasher before the dry cycle and let the warm air in the appliance finish the job. (You may want to hand-dry your glasses.)

Did you know... it takes one 15- to 20-year-old tree to make enough paper for only 700 grocery bags?

Resurrection. Old clothes, towels, bedding and wall coverings never die. They are re-born as brand-new wash rags for your car, home, garden, bathroom and garage.

Oppose disposable. Those wipe-n-toss wash rags are a burden on our waste-management system. A washable, re-usable rag is an eco-friendlier alternative.

Turn down the heat. Everything doesn't need hot water to get clean. You can save over 80 percent of energy use just by using warm or cold water.

Go veggie. Switch to vegetable-based cleaning products. Did you know if every household in the U.S. replaced just one bottle of 28-ounce petroleum-based dishwashing liquid with a vegetable-based product, we could save 82,000 barrels of oil a year? This is enough oil to drive a car over 86 million miles!

> *On average, we threw away around 68 pounds of clothing and textiles last year.*
> Source: Treehugger.com

If you have good Easy Green ideas for cleaning, submit them at **www.EasyGreenBook.com**. Click on the link entitled "The Green Team."

Easy Green Walls, Windows & Floors

> *The Environmental Protection Agency Total Exposure Assessment Methodology (TEAM) studies found levels of about a dozen common organic pollutants to be 2 to 5 times higher inside homes than outside, regardless of whether the homes were located in rural or highly industrial areas.*

Take the "pain" out of "paint." Water-based paints dry faster, include fewer hazardous materials and don't require chemicals for proper clean-up.

Dry, dry again. Let the last remnants of latex paint dry in the can. Once latex dries out, it's non-toxic, so you can feel free to discard your empties.

Turn it on its head. When you're storing leftover paint, seal the lid in place and then store the half-full can upside down. Let gravity help you tighten the seal.

Relocate your paint. If your half-used paint can is too cruddy to properly seal, try transferring the extra paint to another container. Glass is a good choice because you can see what color you're storing.

Give the gift of paint. Perhaps you can't use leftover paint, but someone can. Ask your inner circle of friends, relatives and local organizations. Make it part of the job to find a good home for unwanted paint.

How much energy do we use? Our cars, homes and appliances consume more than twice the energy reserves of Alaska and our Outer Continental Shelf.

Source: Groovygreen.com

To gain is to lose. In the summertime, solar gain (the heat from the sun) is bad. It forces us to run the air conditioning more. So here's the rule: keep windows and drapes closed on the scorcher days. This reduces radiant or passive solar gain.

Windows can account for 10% to 30% of the heating and cooling bill. You can cut these costs by as much as 15% just by switching to energy-efficient windows. Superwindows, which sandwich plastic film between two panes of glass, can cut your bill in half.

Source: "Home Energy Saver,"
Department of Energy

Shade is cool. Use whatever you can to reduce the sunlight streaming into your home on hot summer days. Consider awnings, shade trees or other greenery to keep the sun out.

> If every gas-heated home were properly caulked and weather-stripped, enough natural gas would be saved each year to heat another 4 million homes.

Walk on wool. The tough, plentiful, natural fibers of wool make an efficient floor covering. I know what you're thinking: wool is expensive. That's why you need to go to an outlet that sells remnants. Not only are you completing the recycling cycle (by using wool leftover from someone else's project), you're also getting a bargain.

Carpet tiles. You can buy excess carpet tiles as remnants or mill over-runs. Thousands of these tiles are available at any given moment. You can find them locally or online. This saves you money, keeps the excess out of landfills, and solves your flooring need—an Easy Green triple play.

"Reading about nature is fine, but if a person walks in the woods and listens carefully, he can learn more than what is in books, for they speak with the voice of God."

— George Washington Carver

If you have good Easy Green ideas for walls, windows or floors, submit them at **www.EasyGreenBook.com**. Click on the link entitled "The Green Team."

THE EASY GREEN HOME

Easy Green Renter

Some people think they can't green-up their homes because they don't own them. In that case, talk to your landlords about making the changes. Simply say the changes that you want to make will save money. They'll listen to that. But even if they don't listen, here are a few ideas you can implement.

Insulate. Green renters can put blankets around the water heater. This will save from 10% to 40% in energy and cost.

Caulk. Green renters can seal and caulk air leaks all over the house: windows, doors, fixtures, electrical outlets.

Upgrade. Green renters who own their refrigerators can upgrade to an energy-efficient model, especially if your appliance is more than 10 years old.

Fan. Green renters can choose fans over the air conditioner.

Easy Green. Green renters can also find tips they can use in the chapters in this book about kitchens, bathrooms, bedrooms, furniture, cleaning and gardening. (Not to mention all the lifestyle and investment chapters.)

Roommates are green. Besides saving money and giving you daily company, having roommates makes you greener. You create twice as much waste when you live alone as when you live with three roommates.

Just so you know...Your hot water heater is the biggest energy user in your house. Your home probably generates more emissions every year than your car.

If you have good Easy Green ideas pertaining to roomates, submit them at **www.EasyGreenBook.com**. Click on the link entitled "The Green Team."

THE EASY GREEN LIFE (AND AFTER-LIFE)

Trust me... After you've made some Easy Green changes in your home, you'll want to do more. Here's the beauty of Easy Green: doing more doesn't require more of you. Easy Green is really about living your ordinary life differently.

The section you're about to enter gives you some Easy Green ideas for your lifestyle—your wedding, your pregnancy, your parenting, your birthdays, your holidays—even your funeral. From the womb to the tomb ...everything green.

THE EASY GREEN LIFE

My Big Phat Green Wedding

Once upon a time, everyone wanted a white wedding. Now it's all about a green wedding.

Let me tell you a story. My wife Tammy and I had an outdoor wedding. Exactly one week before the big day, it rained…cats and dogs. Tammy was upset. Let's just say it was not her childhood dream for it to rain on her wedding day. I told her not to worry: if it rained, all that would mean is that we'll think of our wedding day every rainy day for the rest of our lives. That's a romantic notion, but she didn't buy it. Not on her wedding day. Finally the big day arrived—and so did the big clouds. They hovered like a menacing gang. I had to do something. I decided to start a tradition. From now on, in our family, every groom will take a long walk alone on his wedding day, and pray. We'll call it the Walk With God. The idea is that you'll probably need to take one or two more of those walks at several points over the course of the marriage, so you might as well start the habit on your wedding day. Anyway, on my inaugural Walk with God, there was only one topic: the weather. "Please, God, don't let it rain on Tammy," I begged, strolling beneath the scowling clouds. Yada, yada, yada…it didn't work. If anything, the clouds looked worse after my Walk With God. Later, as the ceremony began, I led my groomsmen to the edge of the lawn. Tammy's procession of ladies paraded into position. Then my bride arrived. The harp strummed. The pastor began. Next…a miracle happened—and I swear this is true—in the exact moment I said, "I do;" the clouds parted and sunlight smiled through. Tammy had her dream wedding day. Why? Maybe the Walk With God worked, after all. Or maybe nature was kind to us because we were kind to nature throughout the wedding process. We took advantage of several opportunities to make the green choices. At the end of the day, we had a dream wedding and the earth is better for it. Yes, a wedding is a celebration, a rite of passage, a family tradition, a spiritual event and a dream come true. However, if you're planning a wedding, why not make preserving the earth part of your dream? Here are a few ideas you may be able to use.

Choose an outdoor venue. You save money and energy when the warm sunlight and cool breeze are doing the work instead of the heating and air conditioning units.

Choose a central venue. These days, family and friends are spread out over vast distances. If you choose a place that's central to everyone, you'll conserve gasoline for everyone.

Consider a destination venue. My siblings-in-law Trena and Steven got married in Maui. Yes, that means most of the guests hopped on fuel-hungry airplanes to attend the ceremony, but often you can coordinate travel so that numerous guests board a single plane. Plus, the couple enjoyed their honeymoon and several other relatives took their vacations in the same location that year. So, actually, they reduced the number of flights the family took that year.

Bigger isn't better. Tammy and I were determined to know everyone at our wedding. By limiting ourselves to 140 guests, we saved energy all day long (less electricity for lighting and air conditioning, less gas for cooking, less fuel for parking, less water for everything, less paper for napkins, and so forth.) But, most important, we shared the genuine, memorable, benefits of an intimate wedding: seeing every face; preventing long lines, cramped quarters and annoying waits; enjoying personal conversations with loved ones, rather than speed dating through family and friends. To us, the bragging rights of saying we had a thousand people at our wedding were not as precious as the bragging rights of saying we saw and enjoyed every one of our guests who put forth the effort to make this milestone in our lives into a special day. Plus, we worked the room so quickly that we actually got to sit down, eat, drink, talk, kiss and relax. We actually enjoyed our own wedding, spending most of our time at the sweetheart table for two.

Personal invitations. We literally sent every guest a hand-made, personal invitation. People seemed genuinely moved to learn that their invitations were created by hand by the bride and groom. Making the invitations together also created a fond memory for us as a couple.

Personal favors. We recruited our families to help us make the name plates that sat at every table setting. We did half the work at her family home and half at my family home, adding two more fond memories to our wedding experience.

Recycled invites. If making everything yourself sounds too tacky or too hard to you, then shop for invitations made from recycled paper.

Create a memory band. I'll bet that you and your future spouse have relatives with old jewelry in their attics or in dusty, forgotten cases in a closet or bedroom. Many would be happy to contribute those resources to a "memory band"—a wedding setting to hold your diamond. It's a metaphor in silver or gold: two families blending together to form the foundation for a future family. Your memory band will be a more treasured, more meaningful, more personal piece of jewelry—not to mention, easier on your wallet. And, of course, easier on the planet.

Green wedding gown. Numerous designers are specially designing green gowns. They use natural fibers, recycled remnants or other sustainable ingredients to make your dress beautiful for your earth and your ceremony.

Live your dream. Your wedding is your dream day. No one wants to deny you that special moment in time. If none of the ideas I've mentioned so far sounds right for you, here's the solution: don't do any of it. Your wedding day is YOUR wedding day. Spend your money lavishly, if you have it (or your parents have it). Don't destroy the romance of Your Moment. But…off-set. Contribute to an organization that helps reduce the effects of humans upon the environment. There are numerous organizations devoted to decreasing the carbon footprint that we humans make on the world. Some of them can estimate how much of a footprint your wedding will make and exactly what contribution you should make to off-set that impact on the earth. If that sounds self-serving, then go online to find a calculator that estimates your footprint and separately find an environmental group whose efforts you are willing to support. And make sure your guests know that you're off-setting. Make it clear that, even amid all the extravagance that they just witnessed, you were environmentally conscious.

> *"I recognize the right and duty of this generation to develop and use the natural resources of our land; but I do not recognize the right to waste them, or to rob, by wasteful use, the generations that come after us."*

— President Theodore Roosevelt

If you have good Easy Green ideas for a wedding, submit them at **www.EasyGreenBook.com**. Click on the link entitled "The Green Team."

THE EASY GREEN LIFE

~~~~~~

Hot, Easy Green Sex

There's nothing sexier than green sex. Two fit, firm, freshly bathed bodies writhing in the darkness with the full knowledge that both parties can continue until the break of dawn. How does one achieve this ideal? Read on...

Cardio-foreplay. Sex is rhythm...or more precisely the combination of two rhythms into one. What better way to prepare for sex than working out together. Establish a dual rhythm with your partner on the treadmill, the bike path, the hiking trail, the tennis court—or even the swimming pool. After all, isn't sex a form synchronized swimming on land?

Share the shower. After you've worked up a sweat together with your cardio-foreplay, keep the rhythm going with a romantic shower. If you'd like, sometimes you can start with this step. What a perfectly green prelude to lovemaking: Requires nakedness. Saves water.

Inevitably leads to touching. Sets the mood. And renders both bodies entirely kissable, head to toe. This is such a good idea, it should be a law.

> *"After one look at this planet any visitor from outer space would say: 'I want to see the manager".*

> — William S. Burroughs

Green bed. Organic cotton lingerie, bamboo briefs, and hemp silk sheets. You know the rest...

Delicious sex toys. There's an environmentally questionable chemical often used to soften plastics, such as those frequently used to make conventional sex toys. Rather than debate whether the manufacturing of these toys harms the environment, go natural with your sex toys. Stick to the big four: strawberries, whip cream, honey and the sweet, sweet green meat of the kiwi fruit.

Trash the condom. Flushing used condoms down the toilet can clog up your pipes, bog down local treatment plants and pollute waterways. Throw them in the trash.

Gift-wrap yourself. No gift expresses love as much as giving yourself. Write your lover an original poem or song, or offer a full-body massage, or perform a special dance (with benefits). These gifts are more eco-friendly than buying flowers or something manufactured at an industrial plant or sold in a store. This option is sexy and sustainable...sex-tainable.

Dinner for two. Finish the romantic evening with a light, healthy meal, easily digestible, perhaps with some organic wine to lubricate the mind and prolong the mood.

> *By some estimates, at the rate we are going, the planet's natural resources will only be able to sustain 2 billion humans by 2100. At the moment, 6 billion walk the earth. You do the math.*
>
> Source: Groovygreen.com

If you have good Easy Green ideas for love, sex or romance, submit them at **www.EasyGreenBook.com**. Click on the link entitled "The Green Team."

THE EASY GREEN LIFE

Green Food

"*When we Indians kill meat, we eat it all up. When we dig roots, we make little holes. When we build houses, we make little holes. When we burn grass for grasshoppers, we don't ruin things. We shake down acorns and pine nuts. We don't chop down the trees. We only use dead wood. But the White people plow up the ground, pull down the trees, kill everything. ... The White people pay no attention. ... How can the spirit of the earth like the White man? ... Everywhere the White man has touched it, it is sore.*"

— Wintu Woman, 19th Century

Mmm, mmm, mmm...Green Food

Perhaps the cornerstone of a green lifestyle is having green eating habits. The green movement is intended to nurture a healthy planet. That has to start with healthy people eating healthy food. Hopefully, as we sustain our own health, we'll be more inclined to sustain the health of the earth. In that sense, these next few suggestions are the beginning of it all—the foundation of green living.

Plan healthy meals. Like any improvements in our lives, greener living starts in the mind. You may have to re-define the foods you "love" if those foods don't love you back.

Look for the Big O. The trouble with eating "natural" foods is that no one agrees on what that term means. After all, everybody says the food they sell is natural. Even if it's processed garbage, the ingredients "came from the earth" because…where else would they come from—the farmers market on Mars? We need a meaningful definition for green food. The top nominee is "organic." The US Department of Agriculture (USDA) says "organic" refers to food that's grown without using pesticides, chemical fertilizers, sewage sludge, irradiation, genetic modification, growth hormones or antibiotics." Sign me up! Of course I've noticed that organic food tends to cost more. So it's NOT easier on the wallet. But at least with an official USDA organic seal to guide me, I don't have to read the backs of every package or research the farming practices of every manufacturer. I just look for that "organic" seal. Easy.

Think raw. Raw food is never fried, nor saturated in unhealthy oils or sauces, and consists mainly of fresh fruits and vegetables. And a raw diet conserves energy that would be required for cooking, as well as the energy consumed to transport food (because eating raw often means buying locally raised foods.)

Buy what you need. The traditional grocery list often leads to waste. The over-stuffed refrigerator—and the hoarding mentality in general—are leftover ideas from the Great Depression and other hard times. Let's stop stuffing the fridge with everything we could possibly need for a wide range of meals and start planning what we will eat. Without a specific meal plan, we end up throwing away our spoiled excess, week after week. If you shop with specific meals in mind, most likely you'll buy less, which means you'll spend less—and waste less (and produce less waist). Keep in mind, you may have to shop for certain items more than once every week or two. Fresh, organic and healthy foods don't have the preservatives that allow their packaged counterparts to sit around for days on end.

Make what you buy. All the meal-planning and healthy shopping in the world means nothing if you don't follow through. Find the recipes, prepare the dishes, mix the ingredients for your green diet. Too many of our healthiest meals are sitting in our refrigerators and cabinets unprepared because it's easier to warm up can of soup or TV dinner than, say, to cut up fresh ingredients for a home-made stew. Make a commitment. Those good meals won't make themselves!

Eat what you make. After you've spent your energy and the earth's energy to prepare a healthy meal, don't let it go to waste. Don't let a huge pot of whole-wheat pasta spoil because you're not "in the mood" to eat the leftovers. If you tend to hate leftovers, don't plan to eat pasta for three straight days, don't buy enough to cook such a huge portion, and don't make that huge vat of pasta to begin with. Only plan, buy and make what you will actually eat.

Meatless Monday. I am in search of the perfect hamburger. It's my current restaurant quest. In the past, I have hunted down the perfect steak. I love meat. I will eat meat until the day I die. But not on Mondays. That's the one day a week I choose to never eat meat. Why? Because my perfect half-pounder costs more than I'm willing to pay. Not the restaurant costs…the earth costs. A half-pound of ground beef requires 6,000 gallons of water to produce. Even my fries are less demanding. (You can produce a half-pound of fries with only 60 gallons of water.) Besides the water bill, my half-pounder requires the exhaustion of grain, the use of hormones, the pollution of land, air and water. That's one expensive burger. I can't stop eating meat entirely. I've tried in the past. But I can at least slow down…at least one day a week.

Watch your MPGs. Cut down on your Miles Per Gulp by buying from local food growers. The average grocery item travels 1,500 miles to make it to your supermarket. This process increases the cost to the consumer and to the earth. Food that travels also tends to require more packaging than its locally grown counterparts. Support farmers markets.

Plastic is petroleum. Every time you buy food in a plastic package (or even food you place in a plastic baggie, or carry in a plastic bag), think of the petroleum you're consuming. Look for choices with minimal packaging—or, better yet, no packaging at all.

Bag to the Future. By the year 2020, we'll all routinely bring our empty grocery bags with us to the store. For years, I've been shopping at Trader Joe's, taking home groceries in DOUBLE-paper bags, which I immediately throw away after one use. Finally, I committed to buying one of their reuseable bags on every grocery shopping trip. Within a month, I had enough bags to hold all my groceries. But...I kept forgetting to bring my reusable bags with me, or I decided to go shopping at the last minute and didn't want to drive all the way home just to get my reusable bags. Eventually, I figured out that I should keep the reusables in the car! I promise you: food tastes better when you know it came home in a bag that helps sustain the earth. Step by step—after years of WANTING to do the right thing—I eased into this new Easy Green habit of bringing home my groceries in reusable bags...and now I couldn't be happier. Someday, hopefully in the near future, all grocery stores will sell cheap, sturdy reusable bags like Trader Joe's.

Can you imagine? According to the Sierra Club, we consume close to ONE MILLION TONS of paper bags for groceries every year. We fly through ONE HUNDRED BILLION plastic bags every year.

If you have good Easy Green ideas pertaining to food, submit them at **www.EasyGreenBook.com**. Click on the link entitled "The Green Team."

THE EASY GREEN LIFE

~~~~~~~~~~~~~~~~~~~~~~~~

The Jolly Green Diet

First, a warning: I'm not a doctor. I don't even play one on TV, but I know this is good advice…Don't do anything hasty with your diet just because you care about the earth.

You have to consult a medical professional before you start changing what you eat. We don't want you to harm yourself. And, believe me, you can do harm if you google "green diet" and follow the first program you see. There are loonies out there, looking to make a quick buck on the "green thing." Some of those people don't know what they're talking about. Also, don't try to create your own green diet. Unless you're a trained professional, you're no more qualified than the loonies. Take it easy, get some help if you want to lose weight the green way.

With that said, may I now introduce the next weight-loss craze…the Jolly Green Diet.

The Jolly Green Diet isn't a set regimen, it's a set of principles. No two Jolly Green Diets are the same. Each one is custom designed by you and your medical professional. I'm not going to prescribe a specific diet because that I would be foolish to do that and you would be even more foolish to listen to me. But I will describe the concept of the Jolly Green Diet…its characteristics…its principles. I will answer the question: If there were a Jolly Green Diet, what would it be? We'll begin by breaking down the concept one word at a time: Jolly…Green …Diet:

"Jolly." A green diet should make you happy. After all, a true green diet is healthier for you and the earth at the same time. If your green diet isn't making you happy, then it's just another diet. Add some fun. For most of us, that's the only way we'll stick with the program. This doesn't necessarily mean adding fun foods. It could mean that part of your diet plan is to cook at least one healthy meal per week with someone you love or someone you would like to love better. Cooking together builds a bond unlike any other. If you do this right, you'll end up with a better meal and a better marriage, or a better friendship, or whatever better relationship you crave. The idea is to replace a craving for sweets with a craving for sweetness in your life. Here's the bottom line: You should be happier when you lose weight with the Jolly Green Diet because you know that you're in better shape and the earth's in better shape, too.

"Green." If you and your doctor can find (or create) the Jolly Green Diet, you have the ultimate motivation to stick to it: losing the weight means saving the world. It must be harder to break a "save the world" diet than it is to break a Laguna Beach diet or a South Beach diet. When you're on the Jolly Green Diet and someone asks you what you're doing for lunch, you can smugly reply, "I'm saving the world. How about you?" Another cornerstone of green thinking is balance. Sustainability is about balancing the supplies and demands of the world. So, the "Green" in the Jolly Green Diet demands that your diet achieve a certain balance. Tell your doctor that you're looking for balance in your life (and on your planet) and so you'd prefer to stay away from a diet that emphasizes loading up on this or completely cutting out that. A Jolly Green Diet ought to reduce carbon emissions, landfill overflow, and the drain on natural resources. So tell your doctor that you'd like a diet that uses fewer packaged products, if possible. More natural, more organic, more local produce or products. At the end of the day, you have to listen to your medical professional. Our point here is this: when the doctor asks you what you're looking for, don't say you want skinny thighs or flat abs…say that you're looking for a diet that will do you and the earth some good.

> *Somehow, the United States has less than 5 percent of the total population, yet we consume more than 30 percent of all the resources.*
> Source: Groovygreen.com

"Diet." The Jolly Green Diet should create better eating habits. Too many diets are tough-love boot camps intended to shock you back into shape. Green living is about sustainability, so a green diet should be sustainable…permanent…lifelong. You should be able to continue your Jolly Green Diet after you've shed a few pounds.

So there it is. Go forth and be Jolly! Eat Green! And Diet …for life!

If you have good Easy Green ideas for improving the Jolly Green Diet, submit them at **www.EasyGreenBook. com**. Click on the link entitled "The Green Team."

THE EASY GREEN LIFE

~~~~~~~~~~~~~~~~~~~~~~~~~~~~~~~~~~~~~

Liquid Matters: From Green Water to Green Wine

"*Dis-moi ce que tu manges, je te dirai ce que tu es. (Tell me what you eat, and I shall tell you what you are.)*"

> — French goumet
> Anthelme Brillat-Savarin (1826)

"*Der Mensch ist, was er ißt. (Man is what he eats.)*"

> — German philosopher
> Ludwig Andreas Feuerbach (circa 1863)

"*You are what you eat.*"

> — American nutritionist
> Victor Hugo Lindlahr (1940)

Different philosophers from cultures around the world have expressed the notion that we are what we eat. But it's time we also realize that we are what we drink.

Liquid matters.

This entire section is about the liquids in our lives. Of course, we do more with liquids than just drink them, so we'll talk about all the uses of everything wet from water to wine.

I will begin with a spirited rant about bottled water. Before I begin, here's my confession. I have trouble in this area. For me, the following advice is dark green…difficult green—not light green, not Easy Green. In fact, I may never follow this advice from my own book. So if you see me breaking the rule I am about to utter, do not call me a hypocrite. Call me human.

Wean yourself from the bottle. Bottled water. I drink bottled water all the time. Every day. (In between writing the words you are reading, I'm sipping from a 50.7 FL OZ bottle of water right now!) I drink from bottles at home, at the gym, in the car, on the plane, at work, in my sleep. Why do I do this? Believe it or not, I actually think of bottled water as healthier. It's certainly convenient. But—man!—it's wasteful. I never thought about what it takes to bring me that plastic bottle of refreshment. First of all, it's a plastic bottle. So, you have to ask: where does that plastic come from and where does it end up? You also have to ask: is tap water that bad? (For me, the answer is yes, nevertheless I have to admit that this is a legitimate question.) And, finally, you must ask: Who is benefiting from my addiction to bottles? Bottled water is a multi-billion-dollar business. (Some say it's a $16 billion great lake, others say it's a $22 billion ocean. Everybody says it's really, really, really big business.) How did we all get caught up in this craze? I'm sure one factor is how bottled water is sold—all those ads with the sexy bodies and surreal mountain vistas. For me, bottled water is my connection to world-class athletes. Maybe I can't play pro sports, but at least I can drink bottled water like they do. Besides athletes, every celebrity on the planet seems to hit the bottle. I even saw hard-core, gangsta rapper 50 Cent in a bottled water ad? (Since when did bottled water become gangsta juice?) That's how they built a multi-billion-dollar industry—they've made sure they sell their product to EVERYBODY.

So that's how we got here. But what do we do now? Must we ban the bottle? Is bottled water killing our earth?

I'm quite sure that my bottles of water aren't causing global warming, but I also must admit: when you add everybody's together…well, it's having some effect. We consume and throw away 2.5 million plastic bottles every hour. That's 30 million per day…100 billion per year. Seriously, this is a problem. I really should wean myself from the bottle. I know this. But I'll be honest. I'm not breaking this habit. At least not yet. They say the first step to recovery is admitting you have a problem. So far, I'm stuck on that step. I promise to work on this. Beginning tomorrow. (And now I must sip. Ahhhhh.)

Car wash. I see a poster every time I go to my car wash that says that car washes are better for the earth than an individual washing a private vehicle with a hose in the driveway. Of course, I always think to myself, "Well, that's a self-serving sign. Of course a car-wash owner is going to hang up a sign that says a car wash is the best way to wash a car." Here's the thing: just because they're self-serving doesn't mean they're wrong. Apparently, they have a point. Car washes actually use less water per car than you or I do at home. And car washes treat their used water before dumping it into the ocean. Do you do that at home?

Greywater. I can understand why you don't want to salvage rainwater. That's not Easy Green. You'd have to go out into the rain and strategically position a huge bucket …and then you'd have to figure out what to do with all this water you've collected in the bucket. Exactly how do you use it to water your house plants? Precisely how and where do you store it? How long should you keep it? There are answers to these questions, but they aren't easy answers. They aren't Easy Green.

OK, so you won't salvage rainwater. But perhaps you'll consider salvaging your greywater. That's water that's been used once and is available to be used again without special treatment. Toilet water is NOT in this category. Neither is any water that contains soap or detergents. But your fish-tank water may be. There are 139 million pet fish swimming around America right now. Instead of dumping their dirty water in the sink, why not dump it in the garden? Now that's Easy Green. (Note to self: remove the fish first.)

This is a fact...Only three percent of the planet's water is freshwater suitable for drinking. If every American recycled the freshwater we use for our fish, we save enough freshwater to satisfy one billion people for three days.

Lawn. I've never seen more obvious wastefulness in a home than when I watch someone taking care of the lawn. Haven't we all seen that guy who uses the water hose to push one leaf from his tree, across the grass, down his driveway, over the sidewalk, to the street? Come on, people. We know we're wrong when we're doing it. Let's go primitive. Rake. Sweep. Bend over and pick up. (For more tips, see the chapter in this book about green gardening.)

Fix your faucet. Besides the annoying noise pollution, your dripping faucet is kind of a big deal ecologically. This is hard to believe, but one drippy faucet can waste 20 gallons of water. Per day. That's every day. So that comes to, what, 600 gallons per month? Which is, what, 7,200 gallons per year? OK, that's too much waste. Fixing one faucet is worth the effort. This kind of improvement is what Easy Green is all about. Small changes that make a big difference.

Treat your toilet like the throne that it is. If you think a leaky faucet is bad news, get a load of how much damage a leaky toilet can do. How about this: your leaky toilet squanders 90,000 gallons of fresh water every single leaky month? Are you insane? Call a plumber today. Call now!

Join the Drip Police. After you've stopped all the drips at your home, start a crusade against drips wherever you go: work, stores, restaurants, school, friends' homes —wherever. You should aspire to be more annoying than the drip itself. We will save the planet...one drip at a time.

Green Beer in a Green Bar. Every year, there's something called Green Beer Day at the University of Miami (Ohio). They start drinking green-colored beer at 5:30 a.m. They party hard in Ohio. Across the country, bars dye their beer green every year for St. Patrick's Day. I've had a green beer or two myself, including one on the Southside of Chicago last year. It's fun because...it's beer. But that kind of green beer doesn't do anything for the earth. So that's not what this book is about. This book is about places like Village Pourhouse in New York City. They use recycled napkins, paper towels and toilet paper. They clean with green supplies. They wash their own uniforms, rather than pollute the air by using a service that cleans uniforms in chemicals and delivers them in gas-guzzling trucks. They serve organic wine, spirits and, yes, organic beer. Green beer. They are a true Green Bar. What if this were to become a trend? What if on St. Patrick's Day, bars across America took one step toward making their businesses more eco-friendly? What if Green Beer Day evolved into Green Bar Day—a nationwide or world-wide celebration that meant something good for the environment? I'm surprised nobody in Oxford, Ohio, has thought of this idea. College students around the country can cause this revolution, just by insisting that their local watering holes go green...in some way...for at least one day. Let's do it this year. On St. Patrick's Day. Cheers...for drinking green beers at green bars!

Green wine. The wine industry is going green as a grape. There's the California Sustainable Winegrowing Alliance —a group that's trying to reduce its eco-impact. About one-third of the half million wineries in the state have signed on. The Oregon Wine Board has certified more than 25 percent of its members as sustainable wineries. The Organic Trade Association says organic wine is an $80 million business. That's a tiny swig compared to the overall size of the $20 billion industry, but it's a promising start. The point is: green wine is out there. Order some. If you don't like it, order some more. Find a favorite.

Don't whine. If you've tried organic wine numerous times and are quite sure that you don't like it, then look for wines that use organic grapes.

Green wineries. Consider supporting the wineries— organic and non-organic—that create vineyards that function like a complete eco-system. A little thinking leads to a lifetime of green drinking. There are many ways to think green when it comes to wine. Commit to finding your way. Once you figure out what works for you, then all that's left is the drinking. This is a good example of the Easy Green philosophy: Create easy-to-sustain habits that do not compromise your lifestyle and do not compromise the environment. We will save the planet...one habit at a time.

"To forget how to dig the earth and to tend the soil is to forget ourselves."

— Mohandas K. Gandhi

Green coffee. So you want to green your coffee? Start here: get a mug. Especially if you're a member of the Starbucks Nation and drink coffee ritually every day. Invest in a mug. Commit to it. If you do nothing else, this one change is enough for you to consider your coffee drinking to be adequately green.

Sugar blues. This is not about the fact that those little sugar packets use so much paper. This is not about the health risks you take when you consume typical processed sugar. This is not even about the inefficiency of harvesting and transporting millions of little, inefficient, unhealthy sugar packets around the world. Those are serious issues, but changing all of that is not Easy Green. Here's the Easy Green: stop throwing away the packets you don't use! Put them back. Take fewer in the first place. Use them tomorrow. But, please, promise yourself and the world that you will never just toss them out again. Promise? Awwww, aren't you sweet?

Ashes to ashes, and grounds to ground. Toss your used coffee grounds on the soil in your garden.

> *The United States produces more than 200 million tons of municipal solid waste (MSW) per year. Your share is 4.3 pounds per day.*
>
> Source: Groovygreen.com

Green tea. There's a gadget called a tea infuser that will last you for the rest of your life. You'll never use a tea bag again. Even if that's the only green commitment you make for the rest of your life, they should name a forest after you.

Green gift. If you're not a coffee or tea addict, you certainly know one. Give them tea infusers or coffee mugs. When you hand it to them, mention what you've learned about greener beverage habits. Every time they use your gift, they are reminded to improve the earth with everyday habits. And you both get to feel good about it. How easy is that?

If you have good Easy Green ideas for liquids of any kind, submit them at **www.EasyGreenBook.com**. Click on the link entitled "The Green Team."

Easy Green Parenting

What could be more important than passing along a healthy earth to our children? Answer: passing along the idea that a healthy earth is important. That's what green parenting is about…easy ways to show and tell children that this planet matters.

Green pregnancy. There should be no other kind. Talk to your doctor about doing everything possible to reduce the number of pollutants in your food, water, air and life. There is a great body of literature on this subject. No green parenting is more important than green pregnancy. Get this right.

Think inside the box. I host a television show now on HGTV. Even as a child, I worked inside the box…a cardboard box. My mother always complained that she'd buy us toys and we'd play with the box. Deep down, though, she realized that it takes imagination to see a world of wonder inside an empty box. So, take a lesson from my mother: don't just throw away the boxes your children's toys come in. I barely remember any of my toys from childhood. Really. I remember the boxes. When your children play with the box, don't stop them...let their imagination roam free.

Kid-powered. Remember the old Hoola-hoop? Simple toy. Yes, it's made of plastic, but at least you don't have to plug it in. It uses your child's energy instead of energy from the grid. Get your toys off the grid and your child off the couch.

Pass it on. Buy toys that you can eventually pass along to another child. Instead of teaching your child how to add to the landfills, you can teach green-living and green-giving.

Go old-school. So many new toys are so fantastic they leave no room for the child's imagination. Wood blocks are simple, sturdy toys. Wood is a renewable resource, as opposed to cheap plastic, which isn't. But, best of all, wood blocks can be anything a child can imagine. My nephews are getting green toys from me.

Take the dog for a family walk. Simply walking is a beautiful thing. Think about it: you're exercising. Your children are exercising. Your pet is exercising. You're teaching a love of animals. And you're spending time together as a family. This single act just might be the Holy Grail of green living.

Visit the library. Checking out books instead of buying them is a way of "recycling."

Walk and learn. Go downtown in the nearest big city and take a walking tour. Study the history, architecture or art of the city. There's nothing more rewarding (or greener) than exercising the body and mind at the same time. This is not only a good lesson to teach your children, often this form of entertainment is cheap—or free. Perhaps your only investment will be a good book.

Use stairs. To this day, I use stairs when I can. Not only am I a type-AAAA personality and therefore have no patience, I also know that stairs are Easy Green. Teach this principle to your children.

> *A disposable diaper takes 500 years to decompose.*
>
> Source: Groovygreen.com

Children inherit the earth. A friend of mine was looking for a book that would help him pass along his green values to his child. He wanted a fun book, with a good story, and good underlying nature-loving values. He couldn't find this book anywhere. So he wrote it. "The Day the Trash Came Out to Play" by David Beadle (Ezra's Earth Publishing). I notice that now there are several similar books on the market, including one by Jen Green. How green is that! Buy books like these for your child. Plant the seeds.

Children's green-tertainment. I still remember those nature shows my mom forced us watch. They were so boring. I hated them. Dreaded them. And now I can't wait until the day that I force my children to watch them.

Green juice. How about a sweetened water for kids? Sounds like a nightmare. But Nui Water says they use fruit juice to sweeten their healthy drink. You can too.

Adult green-tertainment. We have a great DVD set that's nothing but grand vistas of the earth. In fact, it's called "Planet Earth" by David Attenborough (BBC). Tammy and I take the entire set on vacations. We also pop it in when "nothing's on TV"—which is practically every day. (Because, let's face it: the only television program that's consistently worth watching is "Designed to Sell" on HGTV.) Children will do what you do more than they will do what you say. If they see you enjoying and appreciating nature—as entertainment, no less—that's what they'll grow up to do. Thanks, mom.

> *"We do not inherit the Earth from our Ancestors, we borrow it from our Children."*
> — Unknown Native American

If you have good Easy Green ideas for parenting, submit them at **www.EasyGreenBook.com**. Click on the link entitled "The Green Team."

THE EASY GREEN LIFE

~~~~~~~~~~~~~~~~~~~~~~~~~~~~~~~~~~~~

Easy Green School

Your green parenting doesn't have to end at home. You can make sure your child gets a lesson in Easy Green at school, too.

Schools recycle. There's a program that pays your child's school to collect cartridges and cell phones for recycling. (**www.GreenSchoolProject.com**)

Green chips. Computers for Schools refurbishes and recycles computers for schools. Either get your child to sign up or tell other parents about it so they can donate to this organization or another one like it.

Green art. Every parent has the same problem. Leftover art supplies that no longer interest the child. Here's what to do: Suggest that every child at your neighborhood school donate those supplies to the school or another organization. Either the children will start using the art supplies or they will learn the value of making a donation. It's good, green parenting either way.

A recycled idea. Suggest that this year all art projects assigned at your child's school should have a theme: recycled art. The children will flex their artistic muscles and learn something about art no matter what you assign them to do. So why not teach them a lesson about sustainability at the same time?

School projects. Imagine if there were monthly drives in your child's classroom: newspapers, clothes, cartridges, etc. No one would be expected to participate in them all, but everyone would be encouraged to find one that they can support. A project such as this starts with one classroom. One box. Brought by one child. To recycle one common item. Everything great starts with one. Be the one to teach your child to be the One.

A-s-k. This is "Easy Green," so I'm not suggesting that you start a committee or even join a movement. That's an activist's role. That's dark green. I'm saying this: At least ask what your child's school is doing to teach and practice sustainability. Parents have power. Your question could spark change. Keep asking until you see change. Then start asking about the progress. Long after your child has left the school, the programs may keep going. It starts with someone raising the issue. It starts with your question. Ask.

"We must protect the forests for our children, grandchildren and children yet to be born. We must protect the forests for those who can't speak for themselves such as the birds, animals, fish and trees."

— Qwatsinas (Hereditary Chief Edward Moody), Nuxalk Nation

If you have good Easy Green ideas for schools, submit them at **www.EasyGreenBook.com**. Click on the link entitled "The Green Team."

THE EASY GREEN LIFE

~~~~~~

Easy Green Teen

"*Young people, I want to beg of you always keep your eyes open to what Mother Nature has to teach you. By so doing you will learn many valuable things every day of your life.*"

— George Washington Carver

Throughout the history of the planet, teenagers have started revolutions, fought wars, fought for peace, raised their voices, and persuaded even the most stubborn of adults to do the right thing.

So teenagers, unite! The earth needs you. Here are a few ideas.

Start a club that saves the world. Every school has clubs. Some are just for fun. Some are for causes. The Green Club would be fun and serve a far greater purpose than the sitting-around-bored club.

Green your life. Maybe the best thing you can do as a teen is to improve your relationship with the planet. Your transformation will set an example for others, give you credibility when you encourage others to "green up," solicit questions about your green choices that may lead to your peers making the same choices, and set you on a lifelong path of sustainable living.

Green your book reports. Why would you present just another book report? Why not take the opportunity to educate your teacher? Remember your teachers will influence other students, hour after hour, class after class, year after year. Just by doing a green-themed book report, you can earn an "A," earn your teacher's respect and influence the generation that follows you to green up.

Green your class projects. If you're working with several students on a class project, you have a captive audience. They have to listen to you. So what are you going to say? See if you can get the group to commit to a green project. Good for your friendship, good for your grade, and good for the planet. Good for you!

Green your class presentations. What's that you said? You have a class presentation coming up? Does that mean you'll be in front of everybody in your class? Oh, man! Talk about something green. Green it!

Green ticket. Next time you run for office at your school, instead of promising longer lunch hours (which ain't gonna happen) or better school dances (another traditional campaign lie), see if you can get elected by promising to make the school greener. Even if you lose, just getting your campaign message out there is a victory.

Be informed. Teenagers are famous for reciting facts. Young minds are strong. At one point, I knew the batting average of every major league baseball player. Mind you, this information changes every day. So I had to re-memorize hundreds of numbers. Every day. I know...kind of a useless talent and a pathetic waste of time. What if I knew as much about greenness? Yep, in retrospect, that would've been better.

If you have good Easy Green ideas for teens, submit them at **www.EasyGreenBook.com**. Click on the link entitled "The Green Team."

~~~~~~

Easy Green Pets

Pets are the new children.

They are receptacles of love, either as placeholders for children to come or children who have gone, or as alternatives to children. Either way, they are part of the family. Given our pets' place in our hearts and their status as representatives of the animal kingdom, it's hard to imagine that they—a part of nature—could be doing anything to harm nature. The problem, of course, is that they mingle with us and some of our influences upon them are not healthy for the earth (or for them, or for us, in some cases). So do not consider the following an attack upon your pet, so much as an attack upon a problem.

The pile of poo. If a population of only 11 thousand dogs produced two and a half tons of poo in one community, according to one study, how much poo do you think our 80 million furry friends create nationwide? All that unscooped poop (and its billions of bacteria) eventually ends up in our oceans...untreated. Please clean up after your pet and properly dispose of the waste.

Double scoop, please. Many pet owners use their pet walks as an opportunity to care for the earth in other ways. They'll pick up trash they find and toss it out with their pets' poop. (Some even scoop the poop with found litter.) You're stooping down anyway, so why not?

The preferable plastic. If you don't want to pick up trash every day, then at least create better trash by using a poo baggie that's made of biodegradeable plastic.

Meatless Mondays. If every dog ate vegetarian once a week, we could save the enormous amount of energy it takes to raise meat. In this case, the savings is equivalent to almost 800 million gallons of gas. Imagine if your pet skipped meat two days a week! (And imagine if you went meatless for a day or two per week yourself!)

Nylon unleashed. Most leashes are nylon. Sturdy. All-weather. Cheap. And bad for the environment. Together, our leashes unleash as many carbon emissions as a quarter of a million households. If we all replace those leashes with organic canvas or another natural fiber, our beloved pets will be living on a much healthier planet.

Don't feed the birds. Some people's "pets" are local waterfowl. There are three reasons not to feed the fowl: they make the birds fat and lazy, the birds stop doing their job in the eco-system, and they don't migrate when they're supposed to, which throws a remote eco-system out of whack. If you'd like a pet bird, there are plenty looking for a good home.

Better bedding. If one out of 10 caretakers replaced their pets' old beds with new ones made from recycled materials, we'd save more than six thousand tons in natural fibers. Wouldn't we all sleep better knowing that?

Go natural. Feed your pet natural treats and food. Use natural grooming and cleaning products. Look for natural solutions to urine burns and kitty-litter odor. The answers are out there. You are the X-factor.

> *More than 5,500 puppies and kittens are born every hour in the United States. That compares to 415 boys and girls per hour.*
>
> Source: Treehugger.com

If you have good Easy Green ideas for pets, submit them at **www.EasyGreenBook.com**. Click on the link entitled "The Green Team."

THE EASY GREEN LIFE

~~~~~~~~~~~~~~~~~~~~~~~~~~~~~~~~~~~~~

Easy Green Wardrobe

"I say beware of all enterprises that require new clothes, and not rather a new wearer of clothes."

— Henry David Thoreau

Food, clothing and shelter. These are the basic necessities. Our essentials. And they are the areas of our lives where we can have the largest and most-lasting positive effects upon the earth. We've talked about food and shelter already. Now let's turn our minds to creating an Easy Green Wardrobe.

Go vintage. The coolest green wardrobe is vintage style. Retro. Old School. Not clothing that hearkens a bygone era...I mean clothes that are actually from another era. It's the coolest kind of reuse on the planet. Style. Individuality. Quality. Class. Vintage clothing is a cool shade of Easy Green.

Shred. Old clothes make new rags.

Give. Your old clothes are new to someone else. Give them away. Either identify a charity or do what I do: I store old clothes in the trunk of my car until I find someone who needs them, usually someone homeless. I drive around. I find someone roughly my size. I tell the recipients that I have gifts for them. I only give away good clothes in good condition. They say thank you. They feel good. I feel good. The earth feels good.

Take care of your clothes. Use cold water to clean them. Air dry. Keep them nice so that later you can give them to someone who lives in a shelter, someone you love, someone who needs them. Or…you can sell them for cold hard cash. Either way, step one is take care of your clothes.

Recycle sneakers. Have you heard that Nike turns old sneakers into some sort of rubbery playing surface? They do. They've been doing it for more than 10 years. It's called the "Re-use a Shoe" program. Don't say you don't want to bother sending old shoes to Nike. Just do it.

Consign. Add this errand to your list every six months: consign your recyclables. You probably have a local consignment shop in your neighborhood. Even if you don't, you have several online. Craig's List and Ebay are well-known options. You have no excuse.

Bamboo fabric. Yes, it's true. They make fabric out of the pulp from bamboo grass. It's lightweight and strong, organic and antibacterial, soft and smooth. Bamboo grows so fast that the earth can easily make more. That's what we call sustainable!

Hemp fabric. Of course, hemp is often associated with its cousin marijuana, so some countries heavily regulate and restrict its use, which makes it hard to find and sometimes costly to buy. Still, it's worth mentioning this organic fabric. Hemp is durable, warm and highly absorbent. Most hemp garments are woven or knit. Perhaps you can accessorize your bamboo wardrobe with some hemp winter wear.

Hang green. Ask your dry cleaners to use eco-hangers—sponsored garment holders that are made entirely of recycled paper. Yes, they have ads on them, so you have to weigh that fact against the fact that those ads make the hangers possible. As for me, I tolerate the ads because I always felt that the one million or so hangers I have gotten from the dry cleaners were a big waste.

> *One crop of hemp grown on one acre of land produces the same amount of pulpable fiber as one acre of 20-year-old trees.*
>
> Source: Groovygreen.com

"Do not trouble yourself much to get new things, whether clothes or friends... Sell your clothes and keep your thoughts."

— Henry David Thoreau

If you have good Easy Green ideas for wardrobe, fashion or fabrics, submit them at **www.EasyGreenBook. com.** Click on the link entitled "The Green Team."

THE EASY GREEN LIFE

The Easy Green R's

We have a lot of stuff on this planet. Sure, we could use more. But, still, we have an awful lot of stuff already. And now, thanks to the internet, we have a better opportunity than ever to get all this stuff out of the wrong hands and into the right hands. For instance, I'm tired of my old laptop. I've had it two years. I want a new machine. This one that I'm writing on is just fine...for someone else. The best part is that "someone else" can be anywhere in the world. We can correspond about my laptop, conduct a transaction, and exchange the money for the laptop without ever speaking. We don't even have to be awake at the same hours. This is a miracle. An everyday miracle. My junk is your joy. Or your junk is my joy. With our technology, we have the historic opportunity to expand the traditional three green R's (Reducing, Recycling and Reusing). If fact, it's time to add three additional R's: Refurbishing, Recharging and Replacing. The following ideas are expamples of the six Easy Green R's.

Buy quality. Here's a new adage: Cheap isn't. Not for you, not for your earth. Buy sturdy, quality goods. Why? Because you can't recycle, reuse, or refurbish junk. We have to dispose of the Disposable Society mindset.

Buy recyclables. You can't recycle things that aren't recyclable. When you make your purchasing decision, include the afterlife of the product in your decision-making. Buy items packaged in paper or glass, aluminum or steel. Stay away from plastic, if you can. Remember, plastic is petroleum.

Recharge batteries. Once upon a time, people illuminated their homes with candles. People don't do that any more. It just doesn't make sense. Once upon a time, people also used disposable batteries. People don't do that any more either. It just doesn't make sense. People use rechargeable batteries now. Right, people?

Recycle cell phones. Just because you're finished with your old cell phone doesn't mean that it's useless. These days, with close to three billion cell phones in use, we can no longer afford to just throw them away. True, your individual cell phone in the trash will not cause a catastrophe, but you can see how throwing away three billion phones is intolerable. Your part of the solution is simply to recycle yours.

Give away instead of throwing away. When you are finished with a recyclable item, donate it, rather than adding it to the waste heap. To make this easy, find one organization that collects recyclables…then you can just send them everything. Easy.

Shred newspaper. Shredded newsprint makes great packing material. Too lazy to shred all that newsprint? OK. Crumpled newsprint makes great packing material, too.

Recycle your peanuts. You know those packing peanuts that come with practically every package that's shipped to you? They're reusable! Keep them in a box. Or donate them. If you don't know where to donate them, google the words "peanuts," "packaging" and "recycling". In 0.1 seconds you'll have about a million answers.

Recycle egg cartons. Usually you can take used egg cartons right back to wherever you got them. Wouldn't it be cool if, one day, you got your own egg cartons back with new eggs?! (Actually, that would be weird, but recycling the cartons is still cool.)

Share the big stuff. Yes! Every household needs its own broom. True! Every household needs its own water hose. Agreed! We need individual trash cans. But do we really need our own chain saws? Couldn't we share certain power tools? Isn't it true that we rarely are mowing our lawns at exactly the same time? I know the suburbs just wouldn't be the same unless neighbors competed for best sit-down mower. Here's a radical idea: Instead of keeping up with the Joneses, why not have everyone on the block chip in for one top-of-the-line mower that everyone shares? (If you must compete, you can compete with other blocks for Best Mower.) I know that some of you can't imagine sharing a lawn mower, but what about hedge clippers, pruners, and fruit pickers? There's no award for Best Pruners, is there? Of course, some of your tools are precious and personal—and that's fine. But please take a hard look at your list and see if there's some major tool you can share with a neighbor or a relative. Every tool the neighbors share is a tool the earth is spared.

Green bling. Jewelry will outlive us all. So why do we insist on brand-new diamonds? Are they shinier? NO! Let's start buying estate jewelry. Let's look at vintage pieces that can be given new life.

Download. The best thing about being alive today is downloading. Well, at least it's one of the best things. It's certainly one of the best for the environment. Loading songs onto your portable music player is SO much better for the earth than manufacturing a CD. And it's cheaper. And it's easier. No driving is involved. No packaging is discarded. And you don't have a disc that will soon be scratched, lost, broken and trash-heaped. (Plus, you don't have to fast forward through all those wack extra songs they cram onto CDs with the good stuff.)

Subscribe to movies and games. These monthly subscription services for movies and games are great if you're an addict. I'm a movie addict. But I cut down my purchases (and therefore my consumption) of DVDs, while actually increasing my consumption of movies. I still watch tons of movies. But I send them back. Then I get more. So, all in all, it's cheaper and easier for me to get more movies. And it's better for the earth. What more can an addict ask?

Think like a thief. Every day thieves strip down and salvage parts from your stuff and mine. They steal from us and sell it piecemeal for profit. Here's my idea: let's strip and salvage our own stuff by recycling, reusing, and reselling whatever we can. We can use the proceeds or savings to help pay for whatever we buy to replace our old stuff.

Packaging is evil. Let's start punishing companies that use too much packaging. If the products are equal, go with the one with the sleek, minimal packaging. It's easier for you to get to your goodies. And there's less garbage for the earth to absorb.

Magazines are reusable. I, unfortunately, fly in a lot of airplanes. That's very un-green of me. But I have to. I live in two cities at once, plus I travel all over the country teaching people how to live greener. (I know there's a thin line between irony and hypocrisy in my case.) But at least my frequent-flying lifestyle has given me a new idea for recycling: take old magazines on the plane and leave them in the seat pocket. If we all did that, we'd save paper, we'd spare our landfills and we'd enjoy our rides more.

Books are reusable. When I'm in Chicago to shoot "Designed to Sell," I live in a downtown high-rise. Those buildings have a great recycling system that I've never seen elsewhere: a book exchange. They place a simple bookshelf downstairs near the mailboxes. When people finish their copy of "Da Vinci Code," they put it on the shelf and exchange it for someone else's copy of "Easy Green." It's like Netflix, except it's free, it's books, and it's a barter system between neighbors in one building. This simple system could be implemented in hundreds of buildings, even thousands of buildings. Every condo complex could put the book shelf in the community room. Every dormitory could put a shelf near the vending machines. High schools could do it. Junior highs. Churches. Offices. Libraries. Bookstores. Bowling alleys. Bars. Coffee houses. Laundromats. The entire system could run on people's honor. Even if someone steals a book, they'll sell it—and that's still reuse! This is a better option than allowing the book to take up space in your home or end up in a landfill. There's absolutely no way to lose. So, in honor of the city where I first saw this system in place, let's call it the Chicago-style Book Exchange. Spread the word.

If you have good Easy Green ideas for recycling, submit them at **www.EasyGreenBook.com**. Click on the link entitled "The Green Team."

THE EASY GREEN LIFE

Easy Green Commuting

Tammy and I were vacationing in Paris with my friends Mark and Jay and their families last year. I found myself admiring French traffic. Seeing hundreds of super-compact cars everywhere you go…you can't help wondering what it would be like if these eco-friendly cars caught on in America. Maybe someday. If you live in certain cities, choosing a car like that seems dangerous, epecially with so many SUV's on the road. Who wants to put their baby seat in a tiny hybrid? Besides the safety factor, many people simply love their big or fast cars in America. They feel that they've earned them, they can afford them, and they don't want some actor or politician telling them that they're destroying the earth by driving the car of their choice. As I promised, my approach is Easy Green. I don't ask you to sell your SUV and start taking the bus. Instead, here are some Easy Green ways you can help the environment in the car you love—whatever it may be.

Keep the pressure up. Believe it or not, maintaining proper tire pressure on your car means a lot for the earth. Your tires will last longer, which conserves natural resources and minimizes harmful emissions, and ensures you better gas mileage. Check your tire pressure monthly.

Warm up on the road. The best way to warm up your car is to drive it slowly on the road. Even in the winter time, no more than 30 seconds of idling is necessary for the engine. I know what you're thinking: Never mind the engine, my car is too cold to sit in during winter. All I can say is: seat warmers. My Chicago car has another cool feature: steering wheel warmers. Newer cars even have heated wiper fluid. Now those are cool, green features!

Tune-up. Fine-tuned engines are fuel-efficient and burn cleaner.

Slow down. I won't lie. I drive a sports car. Actually, sometimes I fly a sports car. (It's a driving machine.) I am not excusing myself. I am confessing. Driving fast is bad. (Sure is fun, though.) If you can, please resist speeding. The difference between 65 miles per hour and 75 MPH is 15% in fuel efficiency. If you sometimes feel the need for speed, make up for it somewhere else in your life.

Ride. Find some way to share a ride with someone other than your family. I tried taking the bus in Los Angeles. I got on the bus at one stop and got off at the next. Maybe the buses are better now, but back then...well, I got off the bus for a good reason. That was years ago and I haven't been back on the bus since that day. However, I have discovered that the "L" train in Chicago is a great way to get from downtown to either O'Hare or Midway airport. Find some way to use public transportation. You'll feel better about yourself. My brother Charles uses public transportation exclusively. He thinks of it as taking a road trip with complete strangers.

Pedal power. Sometimes a bicycle is a better way to get around than a car. (Avoiding the difficulty and expense of parking a car is one incentive to switch to the bike.) But you have to remember to make your bike a realistic option. You will not ride your bicycle until you take it down from the rack in the garage. A bike belongs on the road, not hanging in the garage.

Gas up by moonlight. Always fill your gas tank either before the sun rises or after it sets. At cooler times of the day, your tank will release fewer pollutants into the air.

Recycle tires. Every time you buy new tires—and especially when you buy a set of four—take that opportunity to recycle your old ones. A tire for a tire.

Improve your errand planning. Think through how you should run your errands. Don't make three trips over the course of three days to pick up three items, like I sometimes do. It only takes a minute to plan, or to start a short list. Think twice the next time you're about to run out to the store. Think twice, drive once.

Turn leftovers into takeout. Every once in a while, pack a lunch made from recent leftovers. Or make your lunch fresh and brown-bag on Fridays. Be sure to put a nice note to yourself in the bag like mom used to. This will save you the fuel that you normally use to go out for lunch. If you make this a weekly habit (or, dare I dream, a daily habit), the savings will be significant—for the earth and your wallet.

Stop feeding the leak. Listen carefully…when you drive an older car that has a slow leak, the solution is not to keep adding fluid. Fix the leak. All that oil or transmission fluid ends up in our water.

Replace your cap. How old is your car? More than seven years old? Then replace your gas cap. It's time. By now, it's leaking fumes into the atmosphere even when it's sitting in your garage. That's not safe for you, your family, or your earth. Get a clue…get a cap.

If you have good Easy Green ideas for commuting, submit them at **www.EasyGreenBook.com**. Click on the link entitled "The Green Team."

THE EASY GREEN LIFE

~~~~~~~~~~~~~~~~~~~~~~~~~~~~~~~~~~~~~

Easy Green Traveling

When you stop for food...stop! Idling at drive-thrus is one of the worst things that some of us do every day. On a long driving trip, this faux pas is just too costly. Go inside, stretch your legs, take a break. And give the environment a break.

Vacation locally. You don't have to go away to get away. Discover the beauty around the corner. Pretend you're from somewhere else and plan a get-away to the place you actually live. (Or something like that.)

Choo-choo. Remember dreaming of taking a train ride when you were a child? That was a good idea! Traveling by train instead of car or plane has many advantages. First, of course, it's greener. It's often cheaper. You can get up and stretch your legs anytime you want. You can use your cell phone and other electronic toys as much as you want. No stop lights, speed limits or traffic to worry about, which are the major downsides of car trips . More food choices than a plane. And unlike a plane, it makes sense to plan a trip with several interesting layovers along the way.

Camping. A camping vacation builds character. And think of how much you spare the environment! No TV, no air conditioning, no electric heater, no electric lighting. No electric cooking, no daily laundering of linen, no electric refrigerator, no computer. Of course, for me, this means no fun. But camping is a great idea for a lot of people. Maybe you!

The power of Un—as in unplug. Whenever I'm away from my Chicago apartment, the last thing on my list of to-do's is to unplug everything: the microwave oven, the TV, the printer, the internet phone, the lamps…everything but the refrigerator. Most of these gadgets still suck energy, even when they're turned off.

Green up your hotel room. If there are appliances or lamps or anything that you know you aren't going to use in a hotel during your stay, feel free to unplug them.

Give back. After you've walked through the museum or other attraction, give the brochures, maps, and programs back. You don't need them. Someone else does. If you attend the morning service at your church, give the bulletin back. As a matter of fact, encourage your church to put the announcements on an overhead projector instead of paper. It's easier to make last-minute changes, it removes the printer deadline from someone's weekly duties, and it's better for the planet.

"I went to the woods because I wished to live deliberately, to front only the essential facts of life, and see if I could not learn what it had to teach, and not, when I came to die, discover that I had not lived."

— Henry David Thoreau

If you have good Easy Green ideas for traveling, submit them at **www.EasyGreenBook.com**. Click on the link entitled "The Green Team."

THE EASY GREEN LIFE

Easy Green Holidays

Did you know that we generate an extra million tons of trash each week from Thanksgiving Day to New Year's Day?

Easy Green Christmas

Real tree. You probably assume that displaying an artificial tree is a better for the environment than cutting down a real tree. Surprise! Fake trees are petroleum, whereas real trees are raised on tree farms, and therefore don't deplete the forests. Plus, real trees can be ground into mulch every year and re-used for gardens, parks, hiking trails, playground areas, animal stalls and landscaping. Or they can be used for beach erosion prevention, marshland sedimentation, fish habitats, winter garden decorations, wild bird feeders, and even hazardous chemical clean-ups. So enjoy your real tree: the fresh scent, the authenticity, the ritual, the tradition—and especially the opportunity to recycle.

Take the LED. The greenest Christmas lights are light-emitting diodes (LEDs). The Department of Energy would like to see us all replace traditional holiday lights with LEDs because we'd save at least two billion kilowatt-hours of electricity during the holidays. Give the earth a gift. Get LEDs. And tell your neighbors about them.

Re-gift. Keep those unwanted gifts moving. "Seinfeld" was wrong. It isn't tacky to re-gift, it's green.

Celebrate Easy Green Day. Coincidentally, today is Easy Green Day! Pick one tip in this book that you'll make into a lifelong habit.

Celebrate Earth Day. Today also is Earth Day. (Everyday is Earth Day.)

Send electronic cards. (Just three countries—the United States, Canada and England—together purchase enough Christmas cards to send one to every child, woman and man on the planet.) Besides electronic Christmas cards, I've seen clever cards for Hanukkah, Kwanzaa, Valentine's Day, Rosh Hashanah, Ramadan, Yom Kippur, Diwali, Tu B'Shavat, Groundhog Day, Chinese New Year and Chinese Valentine's Day, Cinco de Mayo, Kentucky Derby Day, Receptionist's Day (I didn't even know there was a Receptionist's Day, but what a good idea!), Flag Day, Bastille Day and birthdays. You get the picture: if it can be celebrated, there's an electronic card for it.

Bring reusable bags for shopping. If you don't have any bags, then re-use the ones from your early shopping trips throughout the season.

Support recycling. If you have an artistic bent, give re-cycled art made from scratched CDs, old wine bottles, last year's Christmas cards or broken dishes. (If you can't imagine making such gifts, you probably shouldn't. There are numerous stores that made tasteful acces-sories out of recycled material: handbags made from misprinted candy wrappers, a jacket forged from plastic soda bottles, backpacks, bookbags and beanbags made from discarded waste. You can find really tasteful, really clever, really green recycled products. If you don't know where to go locally, go online.)

Use party heat. Let the body warmth of your guests heat your home during parties.

Finally, as my gift to you, I've compiled this holiday checklist:

Give living gifts, such as trees, plants, adopted pets.

Buy toys and other electronics that take rechargeable batteries.

Capture your memories with a real camera instead of disposable ones.

Email digital copies of your annual family photo to rela-tives and friends, rather than making prints.

Give your guests cloth napkins, instead of paper.

Clean up after the party with sponges and cloth towels, not disposable wipes.

Break out your real plates and silverware for meals, real cups for egg nog or other beverages, and real silverware for parties and picnics instead of disposable products.

Present gifts in heirloom bags, instead of wrapping.

Buy wrapping made from recycled paper.

Buy leftover wrapping at clearance sales on the day after Christmas and use it all year long, including at the next Christmas.

Open gifts carefully so you can recycle your wrapping.

At least recycle your ribbons and bows.

Make the sweets and gifts, instead of buying packaged products.

Make the dye you use to color your Easter eggs.

Make your costume from vintage clothes or orphaned garments in your own closets.

Attend public fireworks shows.

If you have Easy Green suggestions for Hanukkah, Passover, Ramadan, Rosh Hashanah, Yom Kippur, Thanksgiving or any other sacred day, submit them at **www.EasyGreenBook.com**. Click on the link entitled "The Green Team."

THE EASY GREEN LIFE

Easy Green Hobbies

"Climb the mountains and get their good tidings. Nature's peace will flow into you as sunshine flows into trees. The winds will blow their freshness into you, and the storms their energy, while cares will drop off like falling leaves."

— John Muir

We need hobbies, diversions, escapes. This is a basic human necessity. Green hobbies are not just Easy Green, they are Fun Green. And best of all, they are Guaranteed Green. So search this list for a green hobby that stirs your soul and suits your lifestyle. I've tried to cover hobbies for every part of the world, every season, every terrain, every level of physical ability, every age group, both genders and all ages. You'll notice that I lean toward active hobbies because the idea is to find a hobby that's healthy for you and the earth. Stamp collecting is a fine hobby, but it's not much of a workout. See if you can find your favorite hobby or a new hobby to try.

Archery
Bird watching
Bodysurfing
Bouldering
Canoeing
Cave climbing
Climbing
Crew racing
Deep-sea fishing
Diving
Drawing
Fencing

Did you know that laughter is exercise? A hearty giggle uses 15 muscles in your face and dozens elsewhere in your body. Laughter quickens the pulse, enriches the blood with oxygen and increases respiration. "Laughing 100 to 200 times per day is the cardiovascular equivalent of rowing for 10 minutes."

William Fry, associate professor,
Stanford University

Fly fishing
Hang-gliding
Hiking
Hot air ballooning
Kayaking

Kite-collecting and flying
Lawn bowling
Log racing
Log throwing
Long-distance skiing
Marathon running
Moutaineering
Music

> *Every degree you turn down your thermostat cuts fuel consumption by as much as 10%.*
> Source: Groovygreen.com

Nature photography
Nature study
Paddling
Painting
Portrait Photography
Rafting
Recycled art collection or creation
Recycled clothing design
River rapids rafting
Rock wall climbing
Rowing

> *The United States uses a million gallons of oil every two minutes. Now that's an addiction.*
> Source: Groovygreen.com

Safari
Scrapbooking
Scuba diving
Sketching
Skiing
Snorkeling
Snow shoeing
Snowboarding
Spelunking
Sport fishing
Sports photography
Still-life photography
Surfboarding

> *Did you know leaving your car at home just two days a week will reduce greenhouse gas emissions by an average of 1,600 pounds per year? According to the U.S. Department of Energy, automobile engines release about 19.6 pounds of carbon dioxide per gallon of gas. The U.S. Department of Transportation says that each of the 150 million cars in this country is driven an average of 10,000 miles annually—which means that Americans drive more than a trillion miles every year. Biking is good for your health and the health of the planet.*

Treasure hunting
Triathlon competing
Walking
Whitewater rafting
Wild-life tracking
Yacht charters

All of these hobbies have groups, online communities, regular meetings, vacation packages, literature, magazines, blogs, and podcasts devoted to them. You will not be alone in your healthy hobby. You will find joy and pleasant company, laughter and common ground. And, that, my friends is what green living is all about.

"In wilderness is the preservation of the world."

— Henry David Thoreau

If you have good Easy Green ideas for hobbies, submit them at **www.EasyGreenBook.com**. Click on the link entitled "The Green Team."

THE EASY GREEN AFTER-LIFE

Easy Green Funeral

Death is a touchy topic…an emotional, personal and spiritual topic. So how do I say this discreetly? We use an extraordinary amount of natural resources on funerals. Of course, your loved ones are worth every penny. You should have no regrets. Here is my point: If I'm going to be green in life, I'd like to finish my life the same way. So, for me, cremation is my first option. I prefer that a simple linen or a wicker coffin be used because these take less energy to burn and produce fewer emissions. For others, cremation is not an option. Depending on your beliefs, here are two ideas to consider for a more traditional funeral.

Coffin. They now make coffins from biodegradable materials, such as chipboard and willow. This seems preferable to wood.

Woodland. These days, woodland burial sites are available across the country. These sites are au natural. You don't get a headstone, but you don't disturb nature either. Besides, isn't planting a memorial tree to mark your gravesite a fitting way to honor your green life?

"Shall I not have intelligence with the earth? Am I not partly leaves and vegetable mould myself."

— Henry David Thoreau

If you have good Easy Green ideas for funerals, submit them at **www.EasyGreenBook.com**. Click on the link entitled "The Green Team."

MAKING & INVESTING EASY GREEN

Too often, making green gets in the way of living green.

This need not be.

As it turns out, green and green do go together. Clever folks have come up with green ideas for our jobs and our businesses, our mutual funds and our mortgages. Turn to the next section and say the magic words: give me some Easy Green green.

MAKING & INVESTING EASY GREEN

~~~~~~~~~~~~~~~~~~~~~~~~~~~~~~~~~~

Easy Green Workplace

Being green should be part of the job. Everybody's job. Bring the following ideas to your workplace.

Shut it down. If ten million people in this country turned off their computers at night, we'd keep a half-million TONS of carbon dioxide out of the air every year. This principle is one of the primary cornerstones of Easy Green. If you do nothing else in this chapter (or even in this book), please turn off your work station at night. And when you go on vacation or home for the weekend —unplug.

Hug a mug. Instead of going through an endless line of disposable coffee cups at your job, get a coffee mug that you use over and over. It's much eco-friendlier to wash a mug than it is to manufacture and dispose of those cups.

Screen savers are the enemy. They call them screen savers, not energy savers.

Pretend you're at home. Turn off lights at work when an area is not in use. No, it's not your money being wasted, but it is your earth.

Another bright idea. Use task lighting—targeted lighting that aims directly at the work you're doing—rather than lighting up your entire cubicle, office or other work space. Adjust lighting levels to match different needs at different times. Three-way bulbs will make this easier.

Last one out, turn it off. If you're working late, take a few minutes to power down the coffee machine, copier, printer or whatever other equipment that everyone left on for you.

Think inside the box. Any employee can put a box in the copy room that everyone uses to recycle paper, cartridges and other recyclables. Why not you? You can put another box in place to collect paper to be used for low-priority printing or scratch paper. Just like that, you've made your workplace greener and recycled two boxes.

Start the buzz. I've noticed that some offices are green, while others just aren't. Why is that? I suspect that someone in the green offices has a big, green mouth. They talk about the earth. They encourage others to use the recycling system. They noodge the boss to take recycling seriously. For some people, talking comes easily. If that's you, talk about Easy Green ideas to your co-workers.

Green eyes. Sometimes companies just don't know they're hurting the earth. Managers can't be everywhere and can't see everything. Let's help them. Let's be on the lookout for eco-unfriendly flaws in the workplace: drafty windows, warped doors, unnecessary lamps, and dying lamps (An aging lamp uses just as much power as a new lamp, even though it's giving off far less light).

Know your power. When you see inefficiencies in your workplace, speak up. Or fix them. You'll save your company money, which should help you keep your job, and you'll save the earth. Now that's a good day at work!

Lobby for a laptop. Tell your boss how much better you could do your job with a laptop. They are so much more energy-efficient than desktops that we really should do everything we can to change the workplace norm of buying desktops. Give your boss a business reason to make the switch (besides the fact that laptops save money).

Make scratch pads. A few sheets of scrap paper, a paper cutter and an industrial-strength stapler. That's all you need to make your own note pads. This is a project a child could do on Bring Your Kid to Work Day.

Close the door. You're standing right there...close the door. Wide-open garage and warehouse doors waste heat and air conditioning.

Hold the elevator. It takes just as much energy to carry 11 people to the 14th floor as it does to carry 10. So when you see that person dashing for the elevator, reach over and push the "Door Open" button. Don't think of it as delaying your elevator ride...think of it as saving energy, preserving the earth.

Use the stairs. There's nothing more annoying than holding the elevator for people, only to find out that they're going to the second floor. They should've taken the stairs. Don't be that person. Take the stairs if you're going to a low floor. This rule also applies to people in the low floors of high-rise residences. (I hope all you people on the second and third floors of my apartment building in downtown Chicago are listening. One of you lazy people just inspired this tip four minutes ago. Take the stairs!)

Bug your boss. There's nothing more rewarding than bugging your boss. If your goal is to save the earth, you couldn't be more justified in your boss-bugging. Insist that your workplace go green. Encourage company-wide programs, such as employee car pools, a serious recycling program and overall conservation.

If you have good Easy Green ideas for the workplace, submit them at **www.EasyGreenBook.com**. Click on the link entitled "The Green Team."

MAKING & INVESTING EASY GREEN

Easy Green Business

If you own a business, you have a great opportunity to cut expenses and create your own little green army. You can teach your employees Easy Green techniques that will improve your business, improve their home life, and improve the earth. How can you miss that chance?

Officer Green. Appoint someone in your office to be Officer Green...the chief of the Green Police. Allow them to recruit deputies in various departments. Make this office police force responsible for enforcing conservation policies. Make it fun. Give them badges and green squirt guns. Let them write out tickets. Rotate this responsibility so everyone learns the green policies at your company. The first rule they should enforce: everyone turn off your computer and monitor every night. If American companies made this one change in their employees' professional and personal lives, we could spare ourselves seven million TONS of carbon emissions every year.

"When one tugs at a single thing in nature, he finds it attached to the rest of the world."

— John Muir

Go CFL. Use compact fluorescent lamps and bulbs everywhere you can. Tell your employees that you're replacing the incandescent bulbs to save the company money and to save the earth. If every company implemented this policy and explained the reason for the bulb change, businesses would help spread the word faster about the huge impact that we could make with this Easy Green act.

Windows waste money. Make sure every window is working for you, not against you. (See the chapter on Walls, Windows & Floors for more details.)

Losses and gain. You have a rich source of passive income right outside your window. Passive solar gain. That's the term for heat from the sun. Let the sun come streaming into your place of business and less money will go streaming out to utility companies. You can save on these expenses in the summer, too. All you have to do is open and close your windows when you're supposed to. (See the chapter on Walls, Windows & Floors for more details.)

Be an Energy Star. When you see those words, "Energy Star," you should smile. You are making money on any Energy Star equipment you buy—from computers to printers to copiers. Tell your purchasing managers to make your company an Energy Star.

Buy what you need. The old days of hoarding are over. It's not good business. From now on, only buy equipment, supplies, accessories, gadgets and gizmos that you need. Don't buy just because the purchase looks like a good deal. Maybe your company can afford it, but the earth can't.

Recycling is good business. From now on, think of used paper, exhausted cartridges, spent containers, discarded cardboard, and all forms of plastic, foam, aluminum and glass as a giant check made out to your company. To cash that check, all you have to do is recycle.

Manage your machinery. You don't fire employees just because they have a couple of problems. The same rules apply to equipment, machinery and appliances. Try to fix the problem before you just chuck equipment into the trash heap. Equipment turnover is just as costly as employee turnover. Here's your mantra: repair if you can; replace if you must.

Trade trash. The next time you're at a convention or attending a meeting for one of your business associations, bring up the idea of waste exchange. One business' trash is another's treasure. Smart companies all over the country are bartering garbage. That means they're making money that you are leaving on the table—or dumping in the trash.

Build your business to last. Cheap isn't. Don't cut corners by trying to get away with buying cheap equipment. Purchase goods that will last. You'll save money, effort, nerves, time, and the planet.

Buy in bulk. Purchasing large quantities of products you use all the time saves on packaging, which saves energy, and saves emissions, and therefore saves the planet. Do we have to mention that this also saves you money?

Bring back the company mug. Give your employees a company mug when they join you. It's good for morale. It's good for promotion. And it's good for your business because you eliminate the waste and cost of disposable cups. It's also good for the earth.

Teach employees. Regularly update your employees on what your company is doing for the earth.

Learn from employees. Listen to suggestions for ways you could do more for the earth.

Encourage car pooling. There must be somebody at your business who could share a ride with somebody else. Not only will this be great for team-building, it's great for the air we breathe.

> *For every 1% of our 140 million cars that we tune up, we eliminate nearly a billion pounds of carbon dioxide, which some scientists contend is the key cause of global warming.*
>
> Source: Groovygreen.com

If you have good Easy Green ideas for business owners, submit them at **www.EasyGreenBook.com**. Click on the link entitled "The Green Team."

~~~~~~

Easy Green Investments

With a little research or perhaps as easily as placing a phone call or sending an email to your financial adviser, you can make your savings and investments contribute to making this a better world. There are many ways to green-up your portfolio.

Green mortgage: lower costs...bigger home. There's a little known product called an Energy Efficient Mortgage (EEM), which is also known as a "green mortgage." The idea is that a home with a green design will have lower monthly utility bills. Due to this monthly savings, the same income can qualify for a larger home loan. In this case, it literally pays to be green.

Green mortgage: lower down payment. Another benefit of an EEM is that a buyer can qualify to purchase an energy-efficient home with a lower down payment.

Green mortgage: better home. Another type of green mortgage is an Energy Improvement Mortgage (EIM). This kind of loan enables a homeowner to make upgrades to an existing home that will lower its energy consumption.

Greater eco-value. Because of the ongoing savings of an upgraded home, the energy-efficiency actually becomes a selling point that increases the market value of the home. People will pay more in the short term to save more in the long term. I call that "eco-value." Spread the term. Let's make it a standard term in real estate transactions.

Green mutual funds: There are many investment vehicles designed to appeal to people who care about the environment. Even the Sierra Club has a mutual fund that invests in companies that "consciously attempt to minimize the impact of their decisions on the planet." There are many others out there. The point is that you can ask your financial adviser to guide you toward green investments, if you'd like.

Community investing. Another major movement in green asset management is "community investing," which is designed to put capital directly into green projects.

"The nation that destroys its soil destroys itself."

— Franklin Delano Roosevelt

Divestiture. Some investors have put their money into companies with mediocre or miserable environmental records. These shareholders have the option of letting their money do the walking. By removing their money from the companies' coffers, they send a message: make this company greener...or else we walk.

Shareholder activism. Other investors in eco-unfriendly companies have decided that the best way to fight is from within. They keep their money in the companies, but they demand changes in the companies' behavior toward the planet.

Off-setting. If you ever wonder what effect you and your family are having upon the planet, you can always use the "carbon calculator" found at **www.carboncapitalfund. org.** Once you've determined the size of your carbon footprint, the Forest Service allows you to buy "offsets" through the Carbon Capital Fund. In other words, you pay money to the Forest Service to support programs that off-set the pollution your family is contributing to the planet. You may not be able to decrease the damage you're doing, but you can off-set the damage your home is causing by supporting the worthy efforts of an eco-friendly program.

> *Your family of four generates anywhere from 19 to 30 metric tons of carbon dioxide per year. The Forest Service says the family can offset the damage they're doing with a contribution of $114 to $180 per year through its Carbon Capital Fund.*

If you have good Easy Green ideas for investors, submit them at **www.EasyGreenBook.com**. Click on the link entitled "The Green Team."

A FINAL THOUGHT

〜〜〜〜〜〜〜〜〜〜〜〜〜〜〜〜〜〜〜〜〜

"*The tree which moves some to tears of joy is in the eyes of others only a green thing that stands in the way. Some see nature all ridicule and deformity…and some scarce see nature at all. But to the eyes of the man of imagination, nature is imagination itself.*"

— William Blake

Use your voice. Use your vote.

Perhaps the easiest green of all is to use your influence to get other people to behave greener. That means sharing information that you've learned in this book with your friends and family. That means speaking your piece to people in power.

With friends, family, co-workers and other everyday people, be kind and gentle. Avoid the uglier shades of green: the green guilt trip, the green lecture, the green argument. Dark-green attacks turn off a lot of people. We need those people. We need everyone.

The premise of the Easy Green movement is simple. We'll never get everybody to do everything green, but we can get everybody to do something. Let's make it easy for everyone to join us. Remember: it's always better to do something than to do nothing. So, as you use your voice, draw people in by introducing them to Easy Green and by showing them how profound a difference we can make when we all do our part. Our small part. Our easy part. That's the way to use your voice.

If you want to be a little tough on someone, be tough on the politicians. Send a passionate email to your President, Congressman, Governor, mayor, councilman, or alderman. I'm not saying you should become an activist. That's not Easy Green. I'm saying send an email to someone powerful. Just one email to one politician. Each. If we all did that, we'd see change. Politicians can ignore any of us, but they can't ignore all of us. That's the way to use your vote.

Remember that you also speak (and vote) with your money. Use your power anywhere you spend money. Ask about the green policies at your grocery store. At your apartment. You car wash. Dry cleaners. Restaurants. Make it a habit to ask these two questions: Do you recycle? Why not?

Please, please, please…if you do nothing else the book asks of you, do this: use your voice and use your vote to get others to act. Literally, it's the least you can do.

> *"In the end, our society will be defined not only by what we create but by what we refuse to destroy."*

— John Sawhill

ABOUT
THE AUTHOR

BELMA MICHAEL JOHNSON is entering his sixth season as host of "Designed to Sell" for HGTV. Previously, he has hosted programs for Fox, BET, DIY and syndicated television. This is his fifth published book. As a journalist, he has been published domestically by the Los Angeles Times and Newsweek and globally by the Los Angeles Times Syndicate. He has produced television for Twentieth-Century Fox, Disney, Paramount Television, Columbia Tri-Star Television, Comedy Central, Warner Bros. Television, NBC, the Fox network and CBS/King World, as well as broadband content for TVLand.com, TV-One.com and broadband syndication. As a live entertainer, employee trainer and workshop presenter, he has performed hundreds of times across the United States, the U.S. Virgin Islands and in Canada . He is also creator of WorldwideWritingWiki.com, BelmaMichael. com, EasyGreenBook.com and the forthcoming Lazy-GreenBook.com. He resides in Chicago and Los Angeles, with his wife Tammy. They are expecting twins.

For more information about Belma Michael Johnson, visit www.BelmaMichael.com

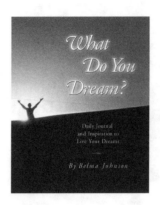

You may also enjoy these DreamBooks titles by Belma Michael Johnson

- "What Do You Dream? Daily Journal & Inspiration to Live Your Dreams" (2001)

- "Write to the Heart: 25 Secrets to Discovering the Writer Within" (2006)

- You can find blogs, vlogs, podcasts, vodcasts, viral videos and who-knows-what-else by Belma Michael Johnson at:

> www.BelmaMichael.com
> www.MySpace.com/BelmaMichael
> www.WorldwideWritingWiki.com
> www.YouTube.com/BelmaJ
> www.Facebook.com
> and www.HGTV.com

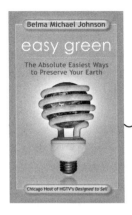

- You can save by purchasing copies of "Easy Green" in bulk for your employees.

- You can commission customized versions of "Easy Green" to serve your company's promotional and educational needs.

- You can add a widget containing a continuous supply of new "Easy Green" content to your website for FREE.

- You can invite the author Belma Michael Johnson to teach your employees and customers the easy ways to green up their work stations, job sites and private lives.

- For more information: EasyGreenBook@gmail.com

**ABOUT
THE HOME DEPOT
FOUNDATION**

FOUNDATION

Building Affordable Healthy Homes

The Home Depot Foundation supports the building of affordable, efficient and healthy homes and the planting of trees in our city parks, on tree-lined streets and in our own backyards. In this way, the Foundation is working to increase awareness of the connection between quality affordable housing, adequate green spaces and trees and the overall health and success of our communities.

The Foundation has invested millions of dollars in communities across the country to help our neighbors of modest means live in homes they can afford to own and maintain in the long term, that provide safe, healthy environments and conserve energy, water and other natural resources.